Maine Beautiful

Maine Beautiful

BY
WALLACE NUTTING

A PICTORIAL RECORD COVERING ALL THE
COUNTIES OF MAINE, WITH TEXT BETWEEN

BONANZA BOOKS · NEW YORK

EXPLANATORY

THE State of Maine is so beautiful, and its wealth of scenery shows such a variety and has such a wide appeal, that the avid American mind will not easily be satisfied with any amount of illustration of the theme.

We should warn all that these pages contain a pictorial representation of beauty spots in Maine, and are in no respect a history. The series of books on the States Beautiful differs in this respect from any other ever published. It has hitherto been considered the proper, and, in fact, the necessary thing, to weave history into illustrated volumes which, in a book of such a character, must be second or third hand, and of no special weight, novelty, or legitimate interest.

The text of this book, therefore, is merely to assist in pointing out the approaches to such beauty spots as we have observed in Maine, and to indicate their peculiar features.

In respect only to the quaint architecture of the state do we deviate from the above scheme. The appeal of good old dwellings is such that they impart a flavor to any series of illustrations, interspersed, as they naturally are, with landscapes. The illustrations in this work are more than nine-tenths new, and are shown here for the first time. The author has made most of them personally. In a few instances he is indebted to the Publicity Bureau of Maine for pictures which for one reason or another it would have been perhaps impossible for him to obtain otherwise, and in such cases credit is given.

The author spent twelve years of his childhood in Maine. As the early years are most formative, especially as relates to the affections, he pleads guilty to a deeper love for Maine than that which he feels for any other state.

The reader, to avoid disappointment, will kindly remember that many scenes, beautiful to behold, are wholly unadapted to the work of the camerist, if we may be allowed to coin the word. The foreshortening of the camera shows, in a manner very disappointing, general and distant views. The many great lakes for which Maine is famous are impossible to show on any plate. If one were to seek to include all the parts of Moosehead Lake, he would require for satisfactory results a mountain rising from the margin to a height exceeding Rainier. It is partial views at best, that we obtain of any subject, and particularly the great features of landscape effects.

Of one other matter we must warn the reader: There are large portions of any state that are not particularly pictorial. We have filled this book with all the pictures our limits will permit. There is a wealth of material ample for other volumes on the same theme. Should we ever attempt another volume, we should emphasize more particularly those parts of the state which are here more lightly passed over.

WALLACE NUTTING

Framingham, Massachusetts

To the

MEMORY OF MY FATHER
ALBION NUTTING
A NATIVE OF MAINE
AND
A LOVER OF BEAUTY

Maine Beautiful

. .

MAINE

THE appeal of Maine to citizens of our country who wish to see nature in her wilder moods, seems to be stronger than the appeal of any other eastern state. Indeed, residents of the remote West also make pilgrimages to Maine, because its wealth of waters supplies a condition of recreation not found in their own part of America. Without being wise enough to indicate all the reasons that call travelers to Maine, it is clear to us that the state supplies nearly all those conditions that please men when they revert for a time, as far as they dare, to the state of nature.

The extent of Maine being about equal to that of the rest of the New England states together, covers a variety of natural beauties such as all those states have, and affords other beauties which they lack. The splendid extent and grandeur of its shore set Maine apart from any other state. The great plains of its northern regions ally it with the praries of the West. Its innumerable lakes, variously estimated in number but certainly running into the thousands, give it unique distinction. The streams that flow to and from these lakes complete the water attractions of the state. The south shore has an antiquity, as regards its settlement, as great as any part of our country. The northwestern portion of the state, however, is as wild and tenantless over great areas as it was in the Indian time. The Maine mountains, while not as numerous as those of New Hampshire, are for that very reason more striking, as some of them rise to imposing heights. The vast Maine forests permit one to roam through their long aisles to heart's content. The orchards and fields are as beautiful as those

7

DRAKE ISLAND, LORD FARM

found elsewhere.   Taken altogether, therefore, there is no feature of
allurement lacking.   What one cannot find in one region is abundant in
another region.   The state is remarkable for its contrasts.

The distance of Maine from the great centers is such that it is free,
generally speaking, from the roistering tripper.   The persons who have
made their summer homes in Maine are remarkable for their independent
point of view.   Here and there at unexpected places one finds a noble site
nobly developed, without reference to the contiguity of any fashionable
resort.   While the north of the state is the paradise of the fisherman and of
the hunter, the high appreciation of the older parts of the state is manifest
in the great number of retired residences, which have taken advantage of
some natural feature like a stream, a lake, a headland, or a forest.

Maine!   The very name inspires a deeper breath and longing.   While
it is true that most travelers are satisfied with the sophisticated centers, we
find that the discriminating seek out in every quarter throughout Maine
those nooks formed by the encircling hills, which supply a retreat, a solace,
and an uplift.

It is not easy to see Maine as a whole.   We know very few persons
who have loved and sought out its various charms.   The predilection of

FLATS AT DRAKE ISLAND

men's minds holds them usually to the admiration of certain charms such as the seashore, to the exclusion of other attractions. To us, the joy of Maine lies, to a large degree, in the differing aspects of its attractions. We love to follow a stream through the smooth clay fields of Maine, where there are no fences and only an occasional decorative maple or elm. We love the bold shore cliffs which here and there remain untenanted. We love the stillness and remoteness of the forests.

THE APPROACHES TO MAINE

THE conventional, we might say the classic, approach to Maine, is by water. Steamers from Boston ply directly to various points of the coast, and one may sail even from New York. The ancient mariners made their historic landings at Pemaquid and elsewhere, establishing settlements which antedate the famous Plymouth landing. For a hundred years, under the Massachusetts government, there were scarcely any roads in Maine. In part, the ubiquitous navigable streams and lakes account for this condition. In part, the clay, which is such a refractory material in its

[*Text continued on page* 19.]

THE PAINTED POOL

By Mildred Hobbs

I know a wooded pool
Where golden lilies lie,
And bathe their faces in the cool
Reflection of the sky.

I've seen it softly kissed
With rose at break of day,
When night's thick trailing robes of mist
Swept silently away,

When Dawn with dainty brush
Flecked opals on the green,
And washed a tint of morning flush
Over the water's sheen.

But O the setting sun!
A mightier hand has he,
Whose strokes of gorgeous crimson run
Into a flaming sea!

He paints the red rocks gold
And silhouettes the pines,
And at his touch the waters hold
The image of their lines.

And what is more like prayer,
Or what more worshipful,
Than heaven's city lying there
Upon the painted pool?

ROUNDING THE CLIFF—ALNA

SEA BARRIERS—MAINE COAST

RECEDING SEAS

SOUNDING SEAS

SEA GULLS ON MAINE COAST

APPROACHING PORTLAND

ADVANCING SEAS—CAPE ELIZABETH

THE WHITE BEARD OF THE SEA

MIDDLE MAINE BIRCHES—NEW VINEYARD

IMPASSABLE BARRIERS

HIGH SURGES—YORK

GATHERING SAP

pure state, is responsible for the lateness of road building. In part, and probably most of all, the sparseness of the settlements has made it impossible to afford good roads in the upper portions of the state.

Approaching by sea, therefore, Portland is the first and most important landing point. Portland, beautiful for situation, the joy of the whole earth, surrounded by the islands of Casco Bay, like gems in her crown, is a fitting city to form the front door of Maine.

The Kennebec River, from Bath to Augusta, is the second main avenue of approach. This stream, throughout its course, and particularly at Merrymeeting Bay, the appropriately named confluence with the Androscoggin, is always beautiful, with green and often high banks, and little cities nestling among their trees.

The Boothbay, Wiscasset, Damariscotta, Rockland, and Camden region, considered as a unit, is marked by an involved contour forming a regiment of points and bays, which meet the ocean like the spears and chariots of an ancient army. Here, also, the coast becomes very bold, and is dominated by mountains which, by their immediate touch with the sea, are most effective, making much of their elevation.

Penobscot Bay, with Belfast, Castine, Bucksport, and Bangor, opens a lordly approach of magnificent dimensions to the rich heart of Maine.

Then there is the dignified and startling beauty of Mount Desert and its environs, and, finally, passing minor attractions, Passamaquoddy Bay, with its tremendous tides, and its opening to Eastport, Calais, and the bordering towns of its fine expanse.

Altogether, no similar extent of shore, here or abroad, can for a moment compare with this Maine coast. In the number of miles of shore line, formed by its involutions, in the heights and beaches, the mountains and streams, the wooded decorations, the safeness of its harbors, and the consequent allurement always accompanying such a coast, the approaches of Maine can never be forgotten by one who loves that mysterious and ever beautiful wonder, the sea. If Maine had no roads at all, it could still afford the summer guest a retreat, delectable and sufficiently accessible for

GREAT CHEBEAGUE, LITTLE JOHN IN DISTANCE

any number of comers. Indeed, there is perhaps as much loss as gain in the improvement of the roads along the shore. Formerly one passed from inlet to inlet, from one peninsula to another, on that free element which has never bowed to a monopoly. There was a freedom, and at the same time a seclusion, in the water approaches to the island and peninsula towns of Maine. An independence and individuality marked the coast dwellers, who developed their admirable characteristics along interesting lines. They were as familiar, in the old clipper days, with London and Calcutta as with New York. They had the broad yet simple outlook of the sailor. Comparison with old world ports, where they must lighter their cargoes ashore, intensified their love for their own incomparable coast, where ships may often safely touch the banks, and where protection from storms blowing from any quarter is available. In their old age, these seamen, often made rich, for that day, by their voyagings, settled in stately old houses which they erected for themselves in scores of little harbor towns. They had the wonderful Maine granite under their feet, and the towering Maine pines, the symbol of their state, over their heads, and their rich lands behind them. Maine is the natural seat of a great marine empire, where one never knows which to admire more, the beauty, or the

FISH HOUSES, GREAT CHEBEAGUE

safety and roominess of the harbors. From the shore, for ages to come, may go out the finest building material, for its stability and gray beauty, that any country can afford; granite. The forests, when properly conserved, as they will be, may supply continuously timber for which the world calls. The country is capable of providing staple food supplies in abundance, and the apples of Maine are delicious beyond any grown in a warmer land.

The brief outline of physical Maine may, and certainly should, interest the visitor. While a shallow idler may be careless of his surroundings, beyond the question of the society and fashion which it affords, a thoughtful citizen adds greatly to his pleasure in a visit to Maine by the consideration that the state has dignity and richness and greatness, aside from its interest as a national playground.

The sea is not only the natural approach to Maine, for persons of moderate incomes, but it is also the most economical approach for persons of narrow means, who, by enduring the simple but cleanly accommodations of the steamers, may be landed in Maine for an insignificant sum. Thus they may enjoy, by careful frugality, a summer rest that does not cramp the remainder of the year.

He who sails his own yacht, however, may visit Maine at whatever expensive figure he chooses to set. All the way from the simple one-man sail-boat to the pretentious steam yacht, the coasts of Maine are followed, at least in summer, by crafts of all sorts. The superior attractions of this coast must in time make it the headquarters of those who wisely seek release from the crowded harbors farther south. There is the additional advantage that the Maine coast furnishes men capable of building and sailing every sort of pleasure craft, however elaborate. The old salt has become a yacht sailing-master.

The land approach to Maine most convenient and most used is the Portsmouth-Kittery bridge. This memorial structure happily succeeds the former obnoxious and noisy toll-bridge. Nevertheless, this great structure, built as it is with steel, cannot be permanent, and any one with an historic or poetic sense must at once feel the inappropriateness of such materials for a memorial. The structure should, of course, have been done in granite or concrete, except for its draw span. The bridge is one more striking evidence of the inartistic temperament of our race. Of course, fifty years from now, when the present structure has crystallized and must be scrapped, it will be replaced by a better form. The road from Kittery through York, Portland, Brunswick, Bath, and Rockland to Bangor and Bar Harbor, is, in some places, of the finest quality, and in certain sections is still in course of improvement. We deprecate the criticism of visitors who forget that a modern highway is far more expensive than a railroad, and that railroads are too expensive to build nowadays. The visitor to Maine may consider that every rod of high-class highway is a gift to him. However much he expends on his journey, he will never repay the state for the advantages he enjoys. The critic often forgets that great cities build nearly all the fine roads. New York and Boston pay heavily for the concrete stretches that run over forsaken areas. Maine lacks great cities. It should be remembered that the total valuation of farm lands abutting on cement roads will not begin to pay the costs of these roads. These things being so, we must be reasonably content for many years with gravel roads, and those not too

THE ENDLESS BATTLE

FOR THE OPEN SEA!

CAMDEN CLOUDS

POLAND BORDERS

YORK BREAKERS

ROUNDING THE POINT—CAPE ELIZABETH

wide. Whatever criticism we indulge should be directed against the parish policy of leaving execrable stretches between fine reaches of good road. The broad view should favor the completion of a good road as far as it goes. It will not be in this generation, nor possibly in the next, that we can look for roads good at all seasons in the Maine counties where no cities exist. Nor may we ever hope for more than a few trunk arteries of permanent highways.

The road diverging from the route we have mentioned at Brunswick, and running through Augusta to Bangor, is designed for another trunk line, which is being bettered from year to year. Main arteries also are mostly completed toward the Rangeley lakes, toward Moosehead Lake, and through the Aroostook and to the provinces. There are also good roads from Portland to the White Mountains.

All roads in Maine are good in the sense of being dry from the middle of June to the middle of July, in the average year. Sometimes the season is extended at both ends for a couple of weeks. If August is rainy, as it often proves to be, the clay roads become a trial to the spirit.

It is highly interesting to see what results from the passing of a cement road by an old farm house, which has been for generations connected with its market town by a slimy slough track. The interest of a traveler over the roads of Maine is, however, more properly centered on the subordinate roads which lead to the hidden beauties of the state. There is more charm in one winding ribbon track than in all the vast extent of state expenditure for highways. For the reasons to which we have alluded, there is no immediate danger of losing the charms that abound on the back roads of Maine. The attractions connected with cultural features are found almost wholly in the southwest corner of Maine, for there alone is seen the quaint architecture which finishes a landscape. Farther north and east we must seek only for natural beauty, and we shall not seek in vain.

The visitor should be warned against disappointment and hasty judgments. He may light upon a Maine county which, while fertile, is singularly bare of picturesqueness. Such regions abound in every state. This

SIR WILLIAM PEPPERELL HOUSE, KITTERY

is so true that a person marked by good judgment in most matters, once
made the statement that there was little beauty in Maine. It is not until
we seek the picturesque that we find Maine to be superior to most states in
this quality. It is necessary to turn off, following the various peninsulas
of the shore, or, in the inland, to seek the hill roads. What more charming short ride than that in North Edgecomb, which leads to the old block
house? The narrow roads about Wiscasset, Damariscotta, and Camden
are often productive of revelations of superb outlines. Skirting the lake
regions, in the lower counties like Oxford, fair scenes are open, capable of
satisfying demanding tastes. One must follow the margins of the bays
and rivers to find what Maine is like. The main road being the shortest
line between large centers, is likely to be of slight interest.

One finds little help by making inquiries. A beautiful road is, in the
thought of your informant, a smooth one. One cannot depend upon the
judgment of the casual citizen. There is, indeed, one sort of beauty which

THE LONGFELLOW HOUSE, PORTLAND

he loves and mentions. He tells you ever of high view-points, and these are worth while. Many such outlooks include great stretches of lake and forest. Beyond that class of views your informant is without information or imagination. He cannot see, until they are pointed out, the intimate and charming compositions which exist in the nooks and curves of valleys and brooks. The delights of the fence corners, of the dells, of the stone walls, are an unopened book. Yet, when he is shown these things in picture, he has the capacity of admiration. As a consequence one must seek for himself the beauties of Maine. This work merely points out such as have appealed to the writer. Doubtless a dozen more volumes, each containing many delightful details could be compiled. As an instance of the numerous fine compositions that abound in narrow range, we venture to state that in the circuit of two miles, from one small Maine village, we have recorded no less than two score of pictures, each almost as good as any we have ever seen. It would not be fair to say that the same could be done about every Maine village. There are numerous bare and uninteresting hamlets. But, given one long summer season, a discerning seeker might readily find two villages every week as entrancing in their environment, and as fruitful in composition, as that village to which we have referred.

The approaches to the northern counties are by excellent gravel roads. But as soon as one passes into the forests, it is astonishing what spaces there are without a dwelling. It is said that across one county by the central, though not the principal, route, there is one house in eighteen miles. This does not at all indicate that the region is not attractive for dwellings, so far as nature is concerned. It merely indicates that in this generation a family is no longer a community, as it used to be, when there were enough individuals in one family to constitute a school. We do not refer, in these remarks, to Aroostook county, where the natural wealth is so great, and the sturdier fashions are so much more generally retained, that the inhabitants have spread themselves more over the land. We remember, however, one road in a county not far from Portland where we were told at a dwelling that it was the last one for three miles. The approaches to Moosehead from various directions are also, in their northern reaches, delightfully quiet solitudes. There is an unique joy in the seclusion of these roads. As Wilfred and I tramped seventeen miles for an especially desirable view of Katahdin, he suddenly broke forth, after a long silence; "This is what I like." We had not seen a dwelling or a human being for many miles. Probably there are myriads of persons who never experienced real solitude, and to whom it would be a delightful novelty. Of course, many persons are distressed by silence. But most of our work, as humans, is so unsightly, so out of harmony with nature, and so ephemeral, that it is good to be where everything remains as it was from the beginning.

It requires, however, a drive over these long woodland stretches to enlighten one who asks why there are not more fine roads in Maine. It is a constant wonder, as we stretch away mile after mile, through the uninhabited forest, how the people of Maine have the enterprise and generosity to give us these delightful thoroughfares.

MAPS OF MAINE

THERE are no good maps of any part of our country. This is of course owing to the rapid development of its cultural features. The best maps are those issued by the government, through the Coast and Geodetic Survey. These maps used to be available by the hundred for a nominal price, and they may still be had by paying a fair rate. When they were issued, they were creditably accurate. That, however, being in most cases at a time when there were no thoroughly good highways, there is no manner of knowing from these maps what the first-class roads now are. Nevertheless, such maps are of the highest value to one who studies seriously in detail any part of any state. Unfortunately they do not yet cover some of the more important sections. The contour lines of these maps are very helpful to the tourist. One sees at a glance where roads reach those sudden dips which are always pictorial; for instance, wherever a body of water lies against a quickly rising hill, there is beauty.

The best general map of Maine is one given for the asking and issued as a matter of advertising. One meets the difficulty, however, that automobile maps seldom consider natural attractions, but devote their attention mostly to hotels. No adequate attention has yet been paid to indicating good roads. One frequently finds an admirable highway where nothing but a single faint line is shown on the map, which line means an impracticable road. Again, various through routes prove to be theoretical, existing as plans only. The ignoring of important features is amusingly shown on one automobile map, which does not even locate Mt. Katahdin, though it is the outstanding feature of interest in Maine for natural beauty and grandeur. The plea may be entered that there is no motor route to its base.

There is room for far better guide books than we possess, but it is a question whether the public would support them, as the best one so far issued, a work of monumental zeal, has not met with an adequate response.

To sum up the helps to finding the best scenery in Maine: *First,* procure the national maps; *second,* procure the motor maps; *third,* check and reinforce the motor maps by the national maps; *fourth,* inquire locally for recent improvements in roads and learn what is at the moment practicable. It often happens that the final main route is at the time impassable. *Fifth,* in the region where there are guides, as in the back country, do not attempt to go alone. *Sixth,* you will find for yourself, more often than otherwise, the beautiful compositions. Leave the roads marked good and keep the ability to walk, by exploring paths. Maine has not been very thoroughly canvassed by art lovers. Artists are inclined to congregate in a few old localities. By far the greater part of the views in Maine are yet to be delineated. Many of them have not even been discovered. We have in this state, near the great centers of population, unappreciated glories, rivalling and often excelling those sought for over the sea or beyond the Mississippi.

THE COAST OF MAINE

THE ramifications of the sea coast of Maine, its extent, and its variety, ranging from gently graded beaches to the bold features of Mt. Desert, make it unique in America. Aside from moderate rocky elevations on the North Shore of Massachusetts, and the isolated out-croppings at Watch Hill, Rhode Island, the Atlantic coast from Maine to Mexico is a practically unbroken low shore. The Geodetic Survey has called attention to this striking circumstance. As a consequence, Americans are beginning to feel that the coast of Maine contains every feature that the heart of man could desire. We are born of a sea-loving, sea-viewing, sea-faring race. Despite the present trend of America away from the ocean, there are still enough of us who love the sea, and all its moods, to hold in increasing appreciation the ecstatic charms unrolling themselves from Kittery to Eastport.

There is another and still more striking aspect of the Maine coast: it abounds in more harbors, perhaps, than the rest of America together possesses. Some of these harbors, like Casco Bay, are to some extent developed. Others, like the regions about Wiscasset, are still very little used. Were there a sufficient number of great arteries leading back from these harbors, they might easily reach a use a hundred-fold greater than now. They lie awaiting the future. They are a constant challenge to the man of imagination. The number of islands and headlands in the bays and straits is legion. They are rock bordered, and some of the very islands themselves are famous quarries. Very recently we have been told by careful students of the subject that granite is the building material *par excellence*. All the edifices that man will ever raise could be supplied with granite of the finest quality from the coasts of Maine.

If we seek farther how these beautiful harbors are to be availed of, we find unlimited lime, sands, and clay, for all the manifold uses to which these basal materials are adapted.

We cannot doubt that the tremendous surge of the tides, which increases as we go eastward on the Maine coast, will some time be harnessed by the wit of man. Hitherto their white manes have escaped untamed. At a time when power is the great focus of civilization, and we are beginning to see the limitations of black and white coal, it is certain that the attention of engineers must more and more be turned toward the limitless power in the tides. Problems more abstruse than the utilization of the tide have been solved. We cannot believe that the genius of America is incapable of taming their power. Once that is done, Maine will become, in con-

[*Text continued on page* 39.]

LOOKING SEAWARD

By Mildred Hobbs

Beyond the bluffs and spray-flung beach
The sea was lost in a silver fog.
At the end of day I sat on an old pine log
With seaward gaze,
And through the haze
The music of a quiet, fog-bound sea,
Like a great mother's crooning, came to me —
The soft antiphony of rhythmic notes,
Deep-throated, from the distant boats,
Low answering high, high answering low;
The lulling, sweet monotony of bells
Swinging slow —
And from the lighthouse glimmered steady flashes,
An eye of warning blinking its red lashes.

As I sat dreaming on the log
And saw the boats returning,
I thought of all the ships we send afar
Named Faith and Hope and Love;
Of how they watch the beacon light,
Those ships of white,
And sail past threatening shoals without a scar.
All treasure-laden they return to us,
With gifts miraculous,
From some far, unseen shore upon life's sea.
But we must never doubt
After we send our white ships out!
They may not bring the prize for which we yearn,
But always they return
Laden with treasure!

LOOKING SEAWARD—NORTH EDGECOMB

DANVILLE BANKS

WHITE BANNERS ADVANCING

SWEEPING CURVES—WOOLWICH-DRESDEN

junction with Nova Scotia, a fountain of wealth for the whole nation. The strategic importance of the state, constructively considered, cannot be overrated. When we remember that the development of power has already exceeded many fold what could be accomplished by all human hands, we may readily deduce the truth of the thesis that civilization depends upon a multiplied application of power. Then, standing on the heights of this picturesque shore, we shall have on the coast of Maine a combination of the picturesque and the practical such as may stimulate the highest faculties of man.

The Maine coast is not merely grand, as are the cliffs of Grand Menan, and as the long beaches like Old Orchard. In its hidden waterways, protected by islands, it possesses numberless quiet stretches of utmost charm. On this coast pour out the fine fresh waters of Maine, the Penobscot, the Kennebec, and the Androscoggin. Those who tire of marine waters only may sail through the estuaries of these streams into a world of splendid beauty, where the green of spring and the flush of autumn spread themselves to the very margin of the streams. There is thus, on the Maine coast and near it, a variety of impressions obtainable, sufficient to entertain the most exacting. It is a far cry from the summer mirror of these little bays, bathed in shimmering sunshine, to the titantic roar and rush of winter waters when they rouse themselves and bombard with terrific detonations the granite bulwarks of the coast. Thus the seasons, the sun, the wind, the contour of the coast line, and its varying elevations, all assemble themselves to supply us with a natural drama, answering to every mood in human experience, and appealing to the gentle, the dreamy, the descriptive, and the tragic. Those who have delineated human passions have failed to explain the strange influence of the natural world on the mind. One thing, however, is impressively certain; that there is great relief for the mind in the moods of the sea. The restless, the forlorn, the tempest-tossed, and even the cynically bitter find help at the ocean's brink. The deep without calls to the deep within. The impression of plenty, of power, and of eternity is conveyed by the proximity of the sea.

Our natural intellectual poverty is challenged by the unbounded mass of the ocean. Our futility is rebuked by the sense that here is an element mighty enough to meet all challenges. Our longing for continuance is fed by the ageless ebb and flow of the ocean's heart. It would seem that power flows into us from the sea. We grow less petty in the presence of this gigantic phenomenon. There is a convincing quality in the great green breakers such that we no longer doubt that what must be done can be done.

But there is a mystic quality in the sea. It holds in its heart so many secrets and hints so constantly at shadowy and wondrous shapes, that its appeal to us is not only physical but spiritual. There is no faculty or department of human nature that is not influenced by the sea. We leap from the ocean to the stars with the greatest ease, and we are stimulated by the mystery and the bulk of the sea to attempt the grasp of mightier things beyond it. Thus the sea has always been a symbol of those vaster and occult powers which lie beyond it, and of which it is the noblest visible expression. The sea seems to connect us with greater worlds. Maine is especially happy in this tremendous asset of its rocky shores. No child is too young, no hoary grandfather too old to be interested and stimulated by the Maine coast. There all ships could find refuge and freights. There all souls can find food enough. There he who peers into the unseen will find a depth sufficiently challenging. There one who wanders from the monotony of the interior plains or the low coasts of the south, and reaches a headland of Maine, feels that he has reached something sufficiently important to engross him, and to fill his dreams.

We love to touch infinity. When we feel the tides touch our feet, we fancy ourselves linked with the infinite. It matters not that we cannot understand deeply the voices of the sea, and the voices beyond at which they hint. As a child listens with a shell at its ear, so the most profound minds listen at the border of infinity. We are grateful for any small echo that reaches us. We feel refreshed by the slightest revelation. While some are content to dream on the shore of the ocean, others launch boldly forth, and either trust or dare its mystery and its terror. They love to feel

ON BOWDOIN'S CAMPUS

themselves at one with the universe. Whether we always formulate our thought or no, we are never fully convinced that the powers which have brought us forth can be dangerous to our being. At least, if we live through battles with the elements, we grow by means of the experience, and in the soul of Victor Hugo we can hear the surge and the wail of the tempest. We love to adapt and to adopt into our own being those features of the infinite which we can apprehend. Nor is it necessary that we should understand in order to benefit by the sea. As a child unwittingly grows through the processes of digestion, so we gain new viewpoints and a better hope and reserve powers by laying our hand on the foaming, tossing mane of the ocean. By what we learn of the ocean, we suspect that we may learn far more. We cannot believe that it has told us any great part of its secrets. Its patient assault of its rock barriers shows no discouragement. Its eternal attack of all the evil things that flow into it, rendering them harmless, may indicate to us that all poisons have an antidote. It is always bringing to us some story of the past. It is always calling us to new journeys and investigations. It is the solace of the poor and the rebuke of the rich. It has something to say to all conditions of men. We are grateful to the sea because it speaks to us in a voice different from that of an ordinary appeal. We are made conscious by the sea that we are yet inarticulate. As what we have said is an echo of what we have seen, it is apparent that we have seen little. If we ask for the classical utterances on various aspects of nature, art, and human experience, we shall find but few of these utterances satisfying, and in some instances there is no utterance whatever that at all meets our sense of what ought to be said. Sailors ought to be eloquent. Or is it true that the multitudinous voices of the sea silence the hearer, teaching him modesty and restraint?

We speak of placing prisoners in solitary confinement. So far as that is concerned, we are all in the dark as to most knowledge, available or unavailable. Men who are never in jail, and indeed are of very lofty character, are yet seeking, and for the most part in vain, to hear and to see the voices and the visions that so slowly unfold for us. The ocean helps to let us out of prison, for we are all bound, hand and foot. Prophets seek to open our eyes and ears and to let us out of our prison house, and thereby they justify their calling as prophets. They are ever showing us something that we have not seen, but might have seen. They are all receivers, who gather from the ether such voices as are ever resonant there, but not available to us in our dullness. Thus the ocean may be to us almost anything that we wish to make it. It is a bathing place or a fishing place. That is something to those who see in it nothing more. To others it is a highway. To others it is a cosmic call. It is the only feature of the earth visibly large enough and mysterious enough to claim all our time and thought.

In this feature, Maine is rich beyond expression. What history, what poetry, what romance, lies latent in the shore of Maine for the coming

FRYEBURG WATERS

PROUD WAVES STAYED

THE BLOCK HOUSE THRO' BLOSSOMS—NO. EDGECOMB

FOREST SIDE BLOSSOMS —FRYEBURG

A TROUBLED SEA—OFF BOOTHBAY

A WISCASSET POOL

A MAINE COAST SKY—CUMBERLAND COUNTY

WHERE THE WAVE BREAKS

FOREST WATERS—DAMARISCOTTA

THE LINGERING SACO

PLEASANT POND—GRAY

A WOOLWICH HOMESTEAD

AN OLD, OLD MILL—ALNA

AN OLD RIVER CURVE—FRYEBURG

generations! To gain our greatest delight, we should think of the Maine shore as the starting point of new epics. What it has in store we cannot tell, but we know that so far its influences are mostly to come into use. As its tides may supply the motive power for our mechanics, so its appeals to our minds and hearts must supply the motive for a fuller literature, based on a richer life. But of this we may be sure: the Maine coast is at present, and for all time is likely to be, the most attractive natural feature of America, except the western mountains; and to those who prefer shore to mountain, the Maine coast is supreme.

MAINE FROM KITTERY TO PORTLAND

KITTERY shares with Portsmouth in forming a natural port unit. Its ancient navy yard and its old dwellings ally it with our pre-revolutionary history. The drive to Gerrish Island is worth while.

York is a large town, with ancient traditions, with its jail museum, and with beach, harbor, nooks, and cliffs, and a river, so that in miniature it contains practically every feature of Maine coast scenery. Its accessibility has made all these features largely available, and it may be thought of as the township in Maine epitomizing, more than any other, the state's shore attractions. For we must not forget that Mt. Desert contains several townships. The communities of Ogunquit and Kennebunkport enjoy the same varieties of coast line, in and out, and up and down, as characterize York. All these communities are supplied with every sort of marine beauty. As the point where the sea and shore meet is said to be the initial point of life on our planet, it would almost seem as if, by a kind of atavism, we hark back to the beaches and the bluffs of the ocean as to the places where we are most at home, and therefore most content.

Wells has its long littoral of quiet outlines. Beaches of the Maine coast are sometimes like those in Florida, being in the form of elongated dunes behind which lagoons lie, most picturesque in their contours. This is true

of Ogunquit, Wells, and Crescent Surf, a portion of Kennebunkport. A
series of islands off Kennebunkport affords a retreat.

The naming of islands is a reflection of many human moods, some of
them humorous. The Maine islands have the usual names repeated after
those of other regions. Nearly all the domestic animals and various wild
beasts are represented. Somewhere in Maine or on the New England
coast we have Sow and Pigs, Ram, Cow, Goat, and doubtless we might go
on with Upper Goose, Goslings, etc. There ought to be a commission
appointed on geographical names. Of course its suggestions never would
be followed, but we would enjoy possessing one more commission — the
substitute for a conscience. At least, however, we might dignify our landscapes by re-naming localities suffering from duplication of names.

At Biddeford and Saco we find the river of which Whittier wrote, the
Saco. The stream has finished its leaps and lazy meanderings and is here
brought down to hard work grinding in the prison house of its dams. At
times, however, to assert itself, the water comes down with overwhelming
flood, and dashes over the natural crags in beautiful confusion. If we could
confine our view to the splendid cascades made here by the Saco we should
be well content. Biddeford Pool is a pleasing detour.

Old Orchard Beach cannot be spoiled even by the unsightliness of its
"culture" features. Its tremendous reach in the form of a flattened
crescent, its great breadth of sands, its limpid, dimpled surface of a
summer's day, and its roaring regiments of breakers in the stormy season,
give it always an interest that does not wane. It is the great beach of
Maine. Scarboro also enjoys a long beach somewhat more removed from
the greater crowds of Old Orchard. And so we come to Cape Elizabeth
forming the southern side of Casco Bay. The endless line of rock coasts,
with here and there a fine bluff, provide a refuge for those who would be
silent and alone. There are combinations of cove and cliff of distinguished beauty. The close proximity of Cape Elizabeth to Portland allows
its development in a more complete manner than could otherwise be the
case. It is enjoyed for many months of the year. Its famous Portland

Head light marks the channel between the Cape and Cushing Island, and is one of the best known points on the Atlantic coast.

Casco Bay, buttressed as it is against the open sea, by islands so over-lapping as to make Portland Harbor remarkable for its safety and availa-bility in all weathers, is a body of water worth all the time one can give to it.

Portland seen from the roofs of its lofty buildings, displays a harbor almost environing the city. Its harbor has been sung by poets and praised by promoters. Nothing too good of it can be said. Our interest, however, is in its remarkable beauty. Portland is the logical point for seeing the best of the east. It is a moderate run, passing by lake, hill, and stream to the White Mountains. It is convenient to Boston, Bar Harbor, and the interior of the state. Its people have adequately met the needs of travelers. The city itself is dignified and beautiful so far as any city at this date in America can be. Its public institutions are of such a character as to engross one during the rainy days. The river park and the near-by suburbs, as ancient Falmouth, and the mosquito fleet for runs in every direction to the large and small islands of its bay, supply the call of an active Ameri-can. Whatever his quest for summer life, he should find it in or near Portland.

The slopes of Falmouth to the sea are of striking beauty. The sea is here, to be sure, but we are still in Casco Bay so that one enjoys the quiet of waters incident to the islands seen some miles out.

Every one of the islands ought to be the seat of a summer home. All this will come in time. The sense of owning a little kingdom, with natural barriers all about it, answers an innate human trait. We can understand the spirit of a man who would rather be king in an island, though he have no subject other than himself and the cat, than to be one in a crowd. The possession of a modern motor-boat entirely changes the situation as regards the ownership of an island. Formerly one was dependent on the moods of the winds or a stuffy steamer. The motor-boat is a close second to its land cousin, the automobile. Can anything be more fascinating than the opportunity of skimming about in a boat among the islands of Maine during the day, and returning to one's own little kingdom at night?

The sea needs no repairs and is never out of commission. During the storms of winter the family may occupy itself in the library, the laboratory, the shop, or the barn. It has been found that periods of vigorous activity, interspersed with periods of repose, carry people onward to success. It is necessary to digest the material acquired by travel and observation. How much we should be enriched if some of the brilliant globe trotters of past centuries had made an occasional minute of their goings and comings! One or two vague or incredible tales are about all that we have to tell us how very early settlers lived in America. It was only after many years that Bradford wrote his simple narrative about Plymouth. Even so, that was lost to the light for centuries. History touching life has been written only at long intervals and at distant spaces.

We wander along the coast of Maine where the earliest houses stood and wonder what their dwellers thought and did. The things which history records are the least interesting. If we could follow a seventeenth-century settler through a season's activities from day to day, it would be far more interesting than any records they have actually left us. If we could know what the early fathers ate, and how they cooked it, according to their own story, and could be told in some homely record of their conversations and avocations, the past and the present could be linked much more closely. It is the tendency in life and history to overemphasize salient features, according to the famous saying, that the nation is blessed which has no history. We are not, however, of that opinion. That rare combination of activity which makes history, and the occasional repose which regards it in perspective can scarcely be found among the early American settlers.

Regarding the dwellings which are erected by summer residents along the coast of Maine, perhaps the less said, the better. In most instances they will fall in the winds. The proper material for a Maine coast house is of course the stones that abound everywhere. We do not mean the

OLD RIVER—FRYEBURG

RIVER KNOLL FARM

SHADOWS ON SAND—FRYEBURG

YORK EVERGREENS

THE ROAD TO THE FORT—NORTH EDGECOMB

A LITTLE MAINE RIVER—FRYEBURG

RIVERSIDE—PORTLAND PARK

OLD DENNETT HOUSE—ELIOT

round boulders such as are in stone walls, which stones were never seen in dwellings in the olden day, and never should be seen in our own. The craze for cobble-stone chimneys, gates, and dwellings is based on lack of thought, lack of taste, and lack of knowledge. The ledges in Maine are in many places broken so as to provide angular stones fit for building. We hope that one hundred years from now the Maine coast may show many thousands of structures resting upon the primal rock, and rising from fragments of the same material. Thus their solidity will satisfy the heart of man, their age will give continuity to the families that dwell in them, and their artistic lines will melt into their surroundings.

Yarmouth has an old-world sound. Its rivers, coves, headlands, have afforded for many years pleasurable summers for tourists. Its Drinkwater Point is most aptly named, especially being in Maine.

One is often astonished, as at Freeport, to know that he is only a mile from salt water when on the main road. If we would see the Maine coast at its best, we must ever follow the rambling, dipping, curving, coast road, which invariably charms us.

At Brunswick the shadows of great elms protect Maine's old classic seat, Bowdoin College, with its fine campus. Here also the rushing Androscoggin makes its last turmoil before sinking into the splendid waters of Merrymeeting Bay. Brunswick is the sort of town one might seek as a residence, especially if he combined scholarly tastes with a love of the country. For here he would be close to Harpswell, Orr's Island, and the endless miles of coast line that border these historic and picturesque locations. Following up the Androscoggin he finds that in its lower reaches it has not altogether lost the charm which it had in its youth at Rumford and Dixfield. The distance to Bath is short, and one is also in line to proceed northerly from Brunswick to the fair banks of the Kennebec, and the region beyond.

If we here follow the shore to Bath, we reach a truly maritime city, with fine past traditions brought down to the present day, of efficient construction in all sorts of sea craft, either for the merchant service or the navy. Here were born many of the clipper ships, and here, even in the last great war, the nation found help for its sea craft construction.

A project for the erection of a great bridge at Bath is now being mooted. We do not object to the ferry, if we have leisure, but who has leisure? At Bath we pass to a region in Maine that has lacked and, as some say, has desired to lack the commercial activity found to the west of the Kennebec.

The highly important estuaries of the Sheepscot and Damariscotta rivers appealed to the earliest explorers of the New England coast so much that they chose these locations in preference to all others. It was at Pemaquid that a pre-Pilgrim settlement of some importance was formed, and at Edgecomb, an ancient fort, whose block-house remains, was erected. There have been dreams of making Wiscasset the Maine outlet for Canada. The deep waters of these estuaries and their high banks seem to the enterprising American to call for a very large development. Meantime, the traveler who loves quiet finds an irresistible attraction in these Maine villages. Wiscasset enjoys a well-deserved reputation for the beauty and quaintness and dignity of its green, and the old dwellings about it. Perhaps there is no other Maine village able to compete with this in the range of its attractions. For the most part it is thought of as a lovely village, but as a center for boating and driving it has a broader and perhaps more important appeal. We found right about Wiscasset and up the Sheepscot and in Woolwich, Dresden, and Pittston, a very great number of compositions containing the elements so dear to the lover of rural life. Woolwich, indeed, fairly belongs to Bath, but as one goes north the western bank of the Kennebec is replete with orchards, quaint early dwellings, minor streams with their little falls, and maple-crested hills for many a mile, even to Winslow, opposite Waterville. Damariscotta has on an estate bordering its inland coves, a wonderful series of birch banks. Its lake, lying a little to the north, and favored by quickly-sloping banks, reminds us of Camden, with its bay and lake, except that here the elevations are not so great.

THE BLOCK-HOUSE, NORTH EDGECOMB

The tide of traffic on this portion of the Maine coast is found farther south on the peninsulas of Boothbay, and those on either hand from it. As we saw over a wealth of cherry blossoms, well on in June, the harbor of Boothbay, we thought the setting was near to perfection. At East Boothbay, also, there is no end of pleasure in exploring the little inlets, some of which have been availed of by tide dams. The entire region with its orchards, farm houses, and shores, allowing one to pass back and forth from the sea to the inland attractions, is most satisfactory. Wandering on through Waldoboro, and Warren to Rockland, we find again, at the last named, a commercial center. It is the first point touched by steamers approaching the wonderful bay of the Penobscot, with its surrounding delights, as at Camden, Castine, and the islands.

We have hitherto adverted to Camden, and have hinted at its excellence. In its harbor, its mountains, and its lakes, it easily maintains a distinction such that one forgets comparisons. They are not necessary. The charm of Camden, looking seaward or landward from its mountains, and the joy of its back-country drives, like those to Union and Washington and Lincolnville, are enough to help us to forget the many things that fill life without blessing it.

Returning to Pemaquid, we find a region of mystery, and therefore of interest. Excavations have uncovered pavements, and pavements, at the beginning of the seventeenth century, mark a very enlightened or very medieval spirit. It would appear that the founders designed to lay out a town of pretensions. It was only by the barest chance that Pemaquid failed to be the Boston of New England. The state has restored the ancient stone block-house, and has thus provided a nucleus for the earliest romance of the east, if we except the mystery of the stone tower at Newport. Investigations at Pemaquid are not concluded. It is possible that more light may yet be thrown upon this primitive settlement.

The location of the North Edgecomb block-house is fine. The old ramparts are in places almost intact. It is a sad commentary on our carelessness of these ancient monuments, that people should be allowed to roam at will about them, cutting their insignificant names in the venerable timbers, and chipping away relics. So fine a monument as this deserves careful protection.

While we are on the subject, we may as well call attention to the remaining block-house at Winslow. It is square, and therefore much simpler than that at Edgecomb, but is more respectably protected. These are the principal relics, in an architectural sense, in Maine, of the ancient time, and a pilgrimage to them, including the natural attractions that lie between, may fill one or two joyous days.

The fine harbor formed in Penobscot Bay by the islands off its mouth is a fitting approach to the river, whose dimensions might almost be called lordly. Running up this stream past delightful old Castine and Bucksport, we reach the fine city of Bangor. In the solidity and attractiveness of its public buildings, and in its natural advantages as a center of the lumbering and agricultural interests of Maine, Bangor is important. It is also the base of extensive water trips northward. The roads center here from the Provinces, from Aroostook, and from the mountain and lake region, of which Millinocket is the second gateway.

One may approach Bar Harbor from Bucksport, crossing the river there by ferry, or may make the longer journey through Bangor. Ellsworth is the doorway of Mt. Desert. It has a fine attraction of its own in Union River, in both directions from the town.

Mt. Desert is so extensive that it includes many sorts of scenery, and in spite of the strong trend of fashion toward it, there yet remain many opportunities for dwellings that need lack nothing in the way of satisfactory outlooks. The center of most towns is the least interesting portion, and this statement is true of Mt. Desert. We have not learned, and probably we may never learn, to combine beauty with business. Not that the combination is impracticable, or even difficult, but it requires a harmonious effort, and long planning in advance. Otherwise the almost total obliteration of a town is necessary before it can be reëstablished on harmonious lines. This, of course, is not to be thought of. It is only in the development of new centers that men of vision may provide for desirable architectural centers.

Mt. Desert is yet, for the most part, free from that fenced-in condition and ever-present sense of hostility which marks Newport. The people of Mt. Desert have manifested fine feeling for the beauty of their island as a national focus of joy. This is a happy circumstance, which we hope will continue as the island develops. A score of years hence the number and the quality of the residences on the island will be such that the importance of the right spirit toward the general public will be increasingly felt.

Passing from Ellsworth and Machias to Eastport, one sees little as yet of efforts to use the coast as an esthetic asset. The region has been lumbered. In process of time, of course, these interesting bays and promontories must come to their own, as the refuge and the solace of weary America. Extensive as the Maine coast is, the greatness of our country will find it not one mile too long. In this latter portion of the Maine coast journey, one passes occasionally estuaries of striking natural beauty. The rush of the tides, coming up to meet the little cascades that are formed at low water, is an unending source of pleasure. At the Sullivan ferry, which, by the way, may be avoided, the present outrageous toll ought not to be tolerated. It is finally to be done away by the completion of a great bridge. Millbridge, Cherryfield, and Jonesboro are the starting points of attractive inland roads, and from Machias one may journey north, omitting Eastport, and threading the lake region to Calais. Eastport, however, should be taken in by everyone, and the interior route may be followed as a side trip. There is room for romance as one sees the stone stairs at Eastport docks, reaching down, down, down, deep beneath the green water. The tremendous tide here offers room for a story by an American Hugo.

PASSAMAQUODDY BAY

FOR more than forty years, since the author while a student enjoyed a wonderful summer on Campobello Island, to the present hour, Passamaquoddy Bay has been a glittering, beckoning memory. It is a fitting approach to our country on the east. Though marred now by the brutal criminality of rum running, its dimpling waters will at last, of course, be redeemed to peaceful beauty. For many miles the Maine shore, indented by hidden bays and the fascinating pagoda shapes of evergreens on the little peninsulas, extends to the St. Croix. At present it is only those who have the discernment to go far and to form their homes by humoring rather than thwarting nature, who enjoy the shores of the bay. We have not seen any computation of the possible power to be developed by the great tidal dam, which exists in dream only, from the region of Eastport to Nova Scotia. Doubtless, however, the power developed could be gigantic, dwarfing any similar impounding of fresh water. Thought of as a future achievement, this project will naturally place Eastport, and the towns to the north, at the center rather than at the edge of things. Happily such a development will interfere in no way with the charm of these waters. The New Brunswick towns, as seen from the Maine shore, have an almost English outline. St. Croix Island lies beautifully embosomed near the shore.

MAINE'S MOUNTAIN REGIONS

IT is perhaps true that the mountain region of Maine is more extensive than that of New Hampshire. This may seem a startling statement. The size of Maine, however, permits a mountain here and there more or less disconnected with any main range. If all the mountain sections were collected, as is true in New Hampshire with the exception of Monadnock, we should have a very impressive mass of mountains. The chief among them is Katahdin. At present the approach to this noble eminence is rather difficult. The best route in is perhaps from Millinocket. It necessitates leaving the motor car and taking a truck, then to a canoe, and finally another truck, and a tramp. Another approach is by way of Greenville and the Ripogenus Dam. A walk of some six miles is ended by a canoe trip followed by a shorter walk. Then it is the canoe again. However, if one wishes a fine view of the mountain he may gain that from the Sourdnahunk. This is the picture which we show.

We arrived on a day of beautiful summer clouds. As one stands on the dam the waters rush out through the gates in broad torrents of creamy foam. Above stands the mountain with its table top, and above that float in the quiet azure the splendid billows of cloud. The contrast between the turbulence below and the serenity above gives a still greater attraction to the river and the mountain. This stream is the west branch of the Penobscot. The mass of Katahdin and its separation from other mountains give it a fine dignity. It is perhaps on this account the most impressive peak east of the Rockies. Its absolute height is almost exactly a mile. We have not yet seen government maps of this part of Maine, but we hope that they may be completed soon. This mountain is one of a series as we pass westward, skirting several peaks until one reaches the Spencer Mountains east of Moosehead. Their elevation exceeds three thousand feet. They are closely allied with Kineo, which, owing to its strategic location, is probably the best-known mountain in Maine except Green Mountain on Mount Desert. The sail up Moosehead Lake from Greenville,

A ROCKPORT NOOK

APPLE AND ASH—CAMDEN

A LITTLE OXFORD RIVER

WINTER SPORTS

THREE SISTERS—BAR HARBOR

A CAMDEN DRIVE

ATLANTIC ROLLERS—YORK

A QUIET SAIL

reached by motor or by rail, is far and away the most impressive experience one can gain from scenery in the interior of New England. The lake is bordered with fine mountains for a greater part of its extent.

We enjoyed a phenomenon wholly new to us. As we passed by the Spencer range we had a drenching thunder shower. It fell between us and the range. On either side of the shower we observed the sun shining. It was a demonstration in physical geography such as we had seen in sketches but never before in reality. The mountains were partly swathed in mist, affording vague and dreamy outlines, and appeared to be the parents of the storm. The remarkable feature was the absence of storm fore and aft of our steamer. As we approached Mount Kineo we found it well below great masses of white cloud, but with the splendid blue predominating. It is an object of grandeur and delight. The sheerer descent is seen from the opposite side. There are about Moosehead other peaks of much beauty, as Squaw Mountain near Greenville. The great extent of lake affording an almost straightaway sail of forty miles, with its innumerable bays and headlands, and its almost perpetual glory of cloud and color, are all a wonderful experience to those who see them for the first time.

THE LAKES AND STREAMS OF MAINE

THE Indian names of lakes, streams, and mountains in Maine are not as difficult as they seem, being pronounced as they are written. At our first knowledge of these names, they furnish not a little humorous comment. At length, however, their pleasing syllables become poetic, and stand for the sweet, wild districts where they nestle or flow, as waters, or dominate the landscape in noble elevations.

Though the number of the Maine lakes is legion, their total area is only sufficient to render them charming. A lake of great extent loses the beauty of winding waters, broken by many peninsulas. There seems to be a very decisive line of opinion drawn between those who regard these lakes as sources of power, and those who regard them as lures for the traveler. If the state insists, as it easily may, that any lands flooded shall previously be carefully cleared of timber, there is no reason why the beauty of Maine should not be conserved, together with its waters. In no case should the flooding of a timbered country be permitted. It can work no hardship to insist on the clearing of timber. The product ought to come near balancing the cost. Every one of us ought to stand strongly against the unnecessary ugliness of dead timbers, forlorn monuments of carelessness or greed, amid the slack waters formed by dams.

The mountains about the Rangeley Lakes are not so lofty, yet afford, in conjunction with the lakes, scenes of noble splendor. One compares the Rangeleys with the English lake country. That country also we have pictured and admired. We feel that the Rangeley region is not a little superior in its beauty as well as in its extent. The Rangeley forests are more interesting. These regions must be considered as a unit with New Hampshire scenery. To the west of Umbagog one is often disappointed by the absence of pine trees near the margins of our Maine lakes. Whenever we do find good forest specimens they are likely to be in a tangle, so that we may view them only in a general way. Here and there we find birches have been left growing on the very shores, for which they have a strong affection. The mountains of Maine and New Hampshire seen from Upper Kezar Lake in Lovell are to be commended as affording a lake setting of grandeur.

About Lake Meddybemps in Washington County, the hills, while of much beauty, do not rise to the dignity of mountains. The fine mountain shores about Camden and Mount Desert are unique in this northeastern American coast in that mountain and sea come together. The inlets between the mountains and Mount Desert some one called the only fiords in America. The statement seems to us very much forced. Certainly on the Pacific Coast in Puget Sound there are fiords greatly surpassing in grandeur any of those in Norway, but it is not necessary to look so far away. The waterways about Wiscasset appeal to us as true fiords. There

are other inlets on the Maine coast where swiftly-descending hills meet
deep water. However that may be, we should not overlook one region
at the expense of another. As one sails up the Penobscot and sees below
one, opposite Bucksport, Mount Waldo and Treak Hill, the latter rises
directly from the water's edge. He finds at the entrance of Marsh Bay
a slope sufficiently high and rapid to be defined as a fiord. In fact the
sail through the Penobscot in daytime or on the borders of morning or
evening unrolls grandeurs never to be forgotten by those who love the
hills. They are much higher and bolder than those seen on the Kennebec,
which gains its attractions through the intimate and tender green slopes.
The great part of the district in Maine, from somewhat west of Augusta,
well on for one hundred and fifty miles due east, is a country just escaping
the dignity of mountains. It is spattered over with fine hills very often
wooded. If one would patiently and slowly thread the farm roads through
this region he would be in a state of continual joy as one graceful contour
after another unfolded itself.

To return to the features of the shore and mountains, let us say that
the outlook from Maiden's Cliff on the north side of Megunticook is of
surpassing beauty, such that we should be at a loss to match it in our
country. While the terrifying and majestic elevations of the Cascade
Range are lacking, there is here on Maiden's Cliff an intimate outlining
of lakes below, and, looking southeasterly to the sea, all together affording
the highest satisfaction. We were happy in our day's visit to this spot.
The view is well known and everywhere used in pictorial advertising literature. It is apparent, however, that visitors to this point are not as numerous
as they should be. The trail is easy for a mountain trail, and is a climb
of only twenty-five minutes even allowing for intervals of rest. The approach is from a farm house on the lake side, which must be sought out
by inquiry since no signs appear. Ascending the main peak and looking
seaward, a wholly different view is unfolded. At our feet lies Camden
Harbor, and well easterly are the elevations of Mount Desert and north-

[*Text continued on page* 84.]

SEEN FROM MEGUNTICOOK

By Mildred Hobbs

Seaward

A bowl of blue with dots of flashing yachts and steamers —
From tiny smoke stacks belching gray
One waves a gay farewell with floating streamers.

The blue breaks into white about her deck;
On, on she sails, to the bowl's distant rim, fainter and fainter;
Out to the far horizon moves a dim, slow-fading speck!

The Coast

Cool curves of beaches smile among the boulders
While, mile upon mile, out of the sea
The mountains rear their heads and green-clad shoulders.

Inland

Behind the mountains sleeping waters hide,
And shielding them from winds at boisterous play,
Megunticook and his great brothers spread their mantles wide.

From high on Maiden's Cliff the islands seem
Like tufted cushions on a glassy floor,
Where gods may rest their wingèd feet and softly dream.

The miniatures of fringing trees reflect
Along the mirrored shores
With unreal, fairyland effect.

And in the blue-green distance of the pines
Glimmer the shining points of roofs
Among the sweep of mountains sketched in billowing lines.

O glorious Camden trails that lead to such a view,
They miss a sight sublime who would not follow you!

FROM MAIDEN'S CLIFF—CAMDEN

AROUND THE BLOSSOMS—WOOLWICH

A BELFAST COVE

KENNEBEC BIRCHES—HALLOWELL

A WISCASSET WATER NOOK

A GRACIOUS HEDGEROW

A MAINE FARM ENTRANCE—WOOLWICH ROAD

COTTAGE ORCHARD—BATH-WISCASSET ROAD

A HONEYMOON RETREAT—DRESDEN

A WELL SWEEP BACKGROUND—LISBON

A BLOSSOMY CURTAIN—ROCKPORT

THE OLD BARN GABLE—LOVELL

SACO BOWS—FRYEBURG

KENNEBEC BIRCHES

Written by MILDRED HOBBS for picture on page 77

On past the dusk of Popham groves
The river lures a sea-worn craft,
Through curving channels banked with fern
To birch-cooled shelters of her coves,

Where clusters of the birches fleck
Their bits of dappling green and gold
On wimpled waters, when the wind
Runs lightly over Kennebec.

Like ladies waving gilded fans
They stand in slender, dazzling groups,
Swishing their trailing autumn robes,
And whispering their winter's plans.

One bends a graceful, snow-white neck
To catch the sunlight in her hair
And watch its yellow glint reflect
In shallows of the Kennebec.

On past the woods, the sunny farms,
And busy, ship-lined shores of towns,
These ladies lure the sea-worn craft
Into their nooks of golden charms.

With whisperings they nod and beck
Along the river's quivering edge,
As low they lean to kiss and woo
The waters of the Kennebec.

easterly flows along the Penobscot River. There is a healthful, and what we hope not a too sharp, rivalry between Camden and Mount Desert. Each has its peculiar beauties, and they are sufficiently different to set off one another. The loftiness of the Camden Range is as impressive, viewed from the sea or from the lakes, as any of our eastern mountain scenery.

At Mount Desert, in the setting aside of a portion of the island known as Lafayette National Park, and the beginning of a road to the greatest elevation on the island, we have a very satisfactory undertaking and accomplishment. Happily it has not been too late in America to secure under national control a great many of our country's landscape glories. The beauty of Somes Sound and of the fine cliffs and headlands of the various parts of Mount Desert has been rather fully disclosed in our travel literature. The island scene on Mount Desert that most pleased us was a foreground of a field of daisies beyond which lay a lake and Mount Green. On the Southwest Harbor shore we also found a daisy field sloping sharply down to the beach, with evergreens beyond. On the east shore of the island is the impressive cliff which is named Cathedral Rock, from the fact that an arch opens behind its foremost buttress. In the sea there is an endless charm as one wanders along the beach at low tide. We were obliged to climb down a rugged way since we happily came upon these cliffs at high tide. As a rule the tide evades us. They tell us that there are two high tides in a day, but our experience seems to contradict astronomy. These fine cliffs, with the water breaking upon them, are of course more impressive than when one walks upon the beach. The caves formed by the erosion of softer rocks are called The Ovens, and are curious massive cavities in the cliffs. Mount Desert has the peculiar distinction of being at once the summer home of leaders in the financial and intellectual world. It would perhaps be a betrayal of Mount Desert to state that its summer mildness is hurt by occasional fogs. But who in the reeking and torrid July in the great city would not welcome a cool fog? The contours of Mount Desert are in general not so bold as those about Camden, but a mountain island ever holds its own fascination. This portion of Maine

is without doubt destined to become completely occupied by seasonal
dwellers. If they prove to have the wisdom not to tame the scenery it
will be a most happy outcome. For ourselves we can never see the appropriateness of city lawns among the cliffs, rapids, and mountain streams.

The vista of Mount Desert, as it spreads itself before a traveler on the
road from Ellsworth eastward, and especially in Sullivan, suggests somewhat a scene in the Greek Isles only that our elevations are beautifully
wooded. The mountain districts of Maine are almost always rich in lakes,
and this affords more than half their charm. There is almost no end to
the cottage sites to be found made up of a hill slope, below which lies a
lake. We observe usually that cottages are huddled on the very bank of
a lake, and not seldom where the highway dust is wafted against them.
The joy of a lake is as much in looking down upon it as in sailing over it.
Since nature has provided so many admirable hill curvatures in Maine it is
high time that their excellence should be recognized.

It often happens that an entrancing feature of lake scenery consists of
the large and small islands that dot the larger lakes of Maine, from the
mere breaking of the surf by a bold rock to the extent of many acres finely
wooded. These islands, or at least several score of them in the Maine
lakes, are still calling to the seeker for independence, quiet, and beauty.
As seen from above, these islands appear, especially in a quiet day, inex-
pressibly beautiful. We almost fear that the universal use of motor-cars
may prevent the development of homes upon these islands. Human
nature, however, is not easily modified, and whatever means of locomotion
there is in store for us, we may safely believe that an island home will
always be attractive. Perhaps in the general development, the islands will
come into their own again, especially since the invention of the amphibious
airplane.

[*Text continued on page* 91.]

THE OLD BACK DOOR

By Mildred Hobbs

Something there is in the lift of a latch
That opens Memory's door,
Something about its friendly touch
Which takes us back to the old home place
That we knew as children and loved so much,
Back to the house whose sheltering trees
Sang us to sleep with the birds and bees.
Near the kitchen garden patch
By the old back door we played;
How the limb of the maple swayed
With the weight of the swing!
And in the spring
There was always a blue-bird's nest in the apple tree
And a chipmunk scampering on the wall.

Do you recall
The fragrance of snowy linen pinned
Secure on the lines and flapping in the wind;
And how to the old back door we brought our pets,
The chickens and ducks and a woolly lamb?
And is there anyone who forgets
The loved house cat and her lively kittens,
Or the rain-barrel where the ducklings swam,
Or the dog's quick barking behind the screens
When the bearded tramps ate their supper of beans
On the cool, stone step, worn low
By the feet of the children of long ago?
Something there is in the lift of a latch
That opens the door of Memory
Where the scenes of childhood reign!
How many a wanderer longs to see
His old back door down in Maine!

BACK DOOR BLOSSOMS—DRESDEN

A COTTAGE SQUARE—LOVELL

CRYSTAL COVE—GRAY

A COUNTRY PARSONAGE—MANCHESTER

AN ABANDONED ORCHARD—MANCHESTER

THE PATH—CAMDEN

ENTERING THE FOREST—NEAR WALDOBORO

OLD MAINE MILLS

MAINE is the paradise of miniature mills. There is a little valley, beloved of our boyhood, where a tannery and a saw mill followed one another on a stream with an interval only sufficient for the little reservoirs between. One can scarcely take a half-hour's run on Maine roads without encountering one or more such mills or sites where they once stood. They were seldom operated the year through, but only at the time of high water. This time coinciding with that in which farm labor was least demanding, the mill was a convenient outlet for energy. The winter was spent in the forest preparing the logs, the early spring in sawing. These little water powers have lapsed into disuse, owing to the modern specializing in the matter of labor, so that one man does one thing all the time, and loses the pleasure and the development connected with variation of labors. What will become of the little old dams is a question that nature is answering for herself. Occasionally, in a rampant freshet, she gives them a shoulder thrust, and the freed waters of the stream babble over their little cascade as they have done for ages. An occasional structure of great strength still impounds a placid pond, on the margins of which the rushes grow.

At the old Coombs' Mills in Augusta, on a gently shelving shore, baptisms used to occur. This mill has survived, and become more important than of yore. We do not connect the sanctifying of the waters with its prosperity. We are far from believing that the righteous are always well looked after on this planet.

Another mill has been for long a source of tan-bark banking, used to protect the farm houses in winter. Here and there an old mill-dam has been utilized for esthetic purposes, to decorate the grounds of a summer place. One and another of the better of these ancient reservoirs has been purchased by power companies, to be drawn upon in seasons of drought. Some of the old dams have sunken to puddles, owing to the cutting away of timber. Largely, such mill ponds are anybody's property, in the sense that they are unused and await the coming of someone to set them to work again or to beautify their banks.

In the olden time the mill was often the only lively spot in a country town, when the farmers were bringing in their logs or drawing away their sawed product. The delicious odors of the boards as they came from the saw, or the fragrance of the yellow meal that sifted down into the receiving tray, linger yet in our nostrils.

It was a period of small enterprises and slow wheels. There was no Minneapolis hum at the old mill-dam. At North Berwick, Ebenezer Hobb had an old water mill which was famed for the fine quality of the meal it turned out, but in another respect it was like the mills of the gods; it ground slowly, so slowly that the meal drizzled down in a minute stream. A farmer from afar came one day with four bushels of corn to grind. Ebenezer got busy. He descended to the lower regions, and jiggled around with the water gate. He came up and jiggled with other controls. At last the old wheel began to growl, like a rheumatic brute. After a short eternity the farmer inquired,

" How you getting along, Ebenezer? "

" Oh, we're doing pretty well. What's your hurry? "

Another interminable interval, then the farmer breaks out,

" Ebenezer, I've got an ox at home that will eat that meal faster than you can grind it."

At that Ebenezer flared up, and retorted,

" I'd like to know how long he could eat it? "

" He could eat that meal," said the farmer, " till he starved to death! "

CANOEING IN MAINE

IT is natural to suppose that Maine, a state of waters, would develop the finest form of the canoe. This supposition is borne out by the fact. The Indian canoe of birch bark, a rather fragile affair, has been sup-

A LITTLE HOME, WISCASSET

planted by a canoe with close set, thin, cedar ribs, and cedar strakes, all covered by canvas. Such a canoe, twenty feet long, weighs about ninety pounds, and is ample for three people with their dunnage. More can be accommodated if necessary, but three is the right number for comfort. This canoe is not too heavy at the carries for two men, the third toting dunnage in a pack.

The shape of this canoe is closely modeled on the lines of the Indian canoe of bark, with a round bottom rather flattened, and with the ends coming together in a quick, sharp, graceful curve. The shape is the embodiment of an Indian dream. We may think that the horns of the moon and the curves of the graceful birch tree, and the crescent beaches of the Maine lakes gave the suggestion. The result at least is perfection. The canoe combines more than any other human creation the practical and the ideal, reminding us of "the perfect woman, nobly planned." For lightness, for grace, for mobility, for its perfect adaptation to its purpose, no device of man has ever equaled the canoe. It is the home of the woodsman for the greater part of the year. Even at night he draws it on shore and, upturning it, has a roof above him. It is his home and companion. More than any other inanimate thing, it is lovable and beloved. We stroke its curves as we pet a fine horse. It is not without good reason that the canoe has appealed, in picture, song, and story, to the minds of those who discovered it full-grown and beautiful, in the hands of the adept Indian, who evolved it. To be at once a thing of perfect beauty and perfect adaptability to use, is true of few human creations. Its very lightness and elasticity preserve it from harm, where a clumsier craft would be smashed. Its very resilience and fragility make it durable. Like the human character it has the power to rebound after a blow, and to bob up serenely, ready for the next bump. Henry Ward Beecher once made a very telling simile, regarding the resilience of the ferry slips. An analogy based on the canoe would have supplied him with a far more apt and telling illustration.

It is highly significant that the old guide gains an affection for his canoe, and thinks it, despite all the battering it has received, better than a new one. Here and there a strake has been broken. Again and again the canvas has been punctured. Never mind. After a few deft repairs, and one more coat of new skin, otherwise orange shellac, the *voyageur* launches forth again, happier than before, because his own feeling and skill have entered into the craft that bears him. It is a monument to his ability as a boatman, and every scar is a kind of notch-stick history of his experiences in the rapids, from season to season. Like a child, none too perfect, it is the best for him because it is his. In winter he renews it, in the other three seasons he paddles it. It is at once his living and his life. It combines poetry and practicality, so that, even if he reads with difficulty, and has not heard of Keats, his life is nevertheless an idyll.

Maine is especially happy, indeed preëminent, in the range that may be covered in a canoe, with an occasional short carry just sufficient to emphasize the rest and comfort of launching again. A seat in the bottom of a canoe is a post of observation, more joyous and more profitable than the throne of a king. The world passes in review before one. The fish leap about one. The birds twitter as one passes. The marks on the stones show the range between high and low water. The mosses on the trees and the direction of the branches indicate the prevailing winds. The keen and experienced guide reads a long history and indulges in sure prophecy, as the canoe glides along. It is a story not read in history, but none the less worth while and delightful.

The canoe has more to do with the development of history in America than has the battleship. The canoe might well be taken as the symbol and seal of Parkman's wonderful histories. For the canoe was the pioneer of European civilization in the west, even more than the prairie schooner or the Conestoga wagon.

When we see a canoe, we live again our childhood with Cooper. This slight, airy affair, begun by the Indian, and finished by the even subtler skill of the white man, is on its way again to the forefront of American life. There are doubtless more canoes now than in the days of the Indians, and their number is constantly and deservedly increasing. Contrary to the supposition of the unknowing, the canoe is a safe craft. One may, indeed, overset it, but the finest forms and implements used by man require delicacy of control, and when so controlled they are safer than more clumsy implements. It takes little practice to gain as great assurance of safety in a canoe as upon the land. One is far more likely to catch his foot in a root than to catch his keel on a rock. The use of a canoe encourages a certain litheness, combined with a daintiness of touch, which reacts upon the mind of the person who acquires these faculties, and gives a sense of power. One feels almost the assurance of a bird in the sky. A construction which is at once a vehicle and a home, which may be used to sleep in or under, to float in quiet water or to dash through cascades, is an achievement into which doubtless many centuries have entered.

The waters of Maine are competed for by the lumbermen, so that until we get into the real backwoods, we do not have the streams to ourselves with the canoes. But even so, it is highly entertaining and sometimes amusing to observe the adroitness of the paddler in overcoming obstacles. Mr. Thornton Burgess, the notable naturalist and writer for children, was telling the author of his experience with an Indian paddler as they approached a boom. Mr. Burgess asked what his guide would do about that. The reply was, "When I holler, you paddle like ——." When they neared the boom, each put his strength to his paddle, and the canoe gracefully mounted the obstacle like a hurdler. The writer, in canoeing on the Penobscot, was carried through a mass of pulp wood, over which the paddler, working alone, easily shot. On one occasion, when we thought there was no lumber near, we felt a rumbling. When we asked Roberts what it was, he said, "Oh, we are just on rollers." We bumped about for a long time among sticks, some of them quite formidable, but with not half the annoyance caused by the mosquitoes. Upsets in rapids do occur, but they are so rare that every one hears about them, and the guide is always chagrined, as it is a point of honor with him to avoid such mishap. He fears the laugh of his fellows more than anything else. The guides acquire an almost uncanny skill in riding the rough water, and in knowing where they are safe. Of course well-known rapids are shot by them so often that they feel as much at home as in a parlor — probably more so.

The delights of the night camp serve to perfect the experiences of a canoe trip, like a luscious bit of ham between sandwich slices. All the joys in life being emphasized by contrast, the evening is never so delightful as when it closes an active day, nor is the day ever so delightful as when we leave the morning camp. All foods are tasty, though it should be understood that the best is not considered too good to take along. Canoeing with a camera has marked advantages over gunning. One is more likely to bring home spoils, and those spoils are more attractive than the eyes of a dead beast. Further, in spite of the number of cameras, it is rare that one is used in the woods. The catch with a camera is more likely to be original than any catch of fish or game.

Though many indulge in rhapsodies regarding the delights of the forest, most human beings love a crowd. Indeed, when among solitudes we often feel a bit selfish that we should have several square miles to our individual selves. A new train of reflections is suggested. The uninhabited parts of the earth are still very extensive. Its surface, if we ignore the water, which we decidedly are not doing at the present time, still affords some fifty acres to a family! Practically, however, if a man wants room, there are so many ready to resign it to him that he may easily acquire several square miles for the price of a diamond of moderate size. A certain gentleman has been adversely criticised because he acquired an island many miles in extent. Since no one else wanted it, we see no reason to object to his ambition. Some may enjoy canoeing where there are many canoes. Give us the wild! Let us move over the mirrored surfaces where the call of the moose or the loon is the only break in the celestial silence.

There are stretches of hundreds of miles in extent in Maine, like the Allagash River trip, during which one scarcely sees a human being. Yet the sense of loneliness never descends on a true canoeist.

The canoe, in fact, is the only available means of seeing Maine over a great part of its extent. Some years ago, we contributed an article on the fitting up of an old street car with a canoe slung in the clerestory. By negotiation the car was taken in tow to interesting points, and there derailed, and the canoe made use of. Since that time the motor car has made much more elastic a similar plan. By carrying a canoe thus on a specially constructed body, one may live on a motor car with day trips by canoe. We commend this suggestion to those who would like to do it first and report. It is an adventure that we propose entering upon at the first opportunity. When the newness of motoring passes, Americans may return to the water as the more pleasing and the safer recreation. The water is much softer to fall upon than are stone roads.

Canoeing for man and wife, or for a tourist and his guide, offers such a variety of attractions that it must increase, if, indeed, the spirit of freedom still stirs in the blood of Americans. Three-quarters of the state of Maine is an area as perfect as any in existence for this incomparably attractive recreation. Aroostook, Piscataquis, Somerset, and Penobscot counties in the north, Washington county in the east, Kennebec in the center, and Cumberland and Oxford in the West, possibly in the order in which we have named them, offer the widest series of attractions. To us the streams and the small lakes are not only most beautiful, but in other respects most alluring. We would, however, not convey an impression that a long or a strange trip is safe without a guide. The very independence and freedom of spirit which induces men to make canoe journeys, also sometimes induces them to venture too far and to depend wholly on their own wisdom. This is just as dangerous as it is to buy antiques without advice, or after advice.

On a canoe journey, one should frankly dispense with the usual paraphernalia of civilization, and dress precisely as a woodsman does. This remark is especially pertinent to footwear, including heavy, home-knit socks. Otherwise what might be a delightful journey may be very annoying. Those who must keep all the finical aids of the city will not enjoy a canoe journey. Beyond the comfort of a shave, and a dip in the summer streams, one should think of nothing personal.

A great surprise awaited the writer, who found that in the open he could tramp three times the distance that he could walk in town. Dwelling beneath the sky is the only true elixir of youth. A trip of this sort derives additional attraction from a knowledge, at least in a moderate degree, of the trees and shrubs and flowers. The little creatures of the wood, and the game one occasionally comes upon, increase our pleasure.

One confession, however, we have to make, humiliating though it be. Always in country journeys we take a stock of blank paper, to enroll the thoughts that rush upon us. Always all the paper is brought back as blank as at the beginning. The rushing thoughts are drowned or blown away! They seem very important at the time, but while a black fly is crawling through one's hair, or the glory of a summer cloud is overhead, how can one stop to write? Except to a few geniuses like Thoreau, whose memory was perhaps phenomenal, the woods are not productive of literary

MAINE IN SPRING—WISCASSET

A CAMDEN ELM ROW

GREAT ELMS OF RANDOLPH

SEAWARD—NORTH EDGECOMB

UNDER AN OAK BOUGH—EAST BOOTHBAY

OVER THE FIELD ROAD—DRESDEN

SWEET WATER CASCADE—WALDOBORO

achievement. Even artists in oil, if the truth is to be blazed abroad, frequently whisk away, when there is a knock at the door, the photographs of the scenes they are " painting from nature."

THE TREES OF MAINE

WE suspect that when Maine was called the Pine Tree State, the word pine was made to do duty in a general way for evergreens. We know that much furniture, said to be pine, is often spruce or cedar in parts. There is a loose manner of thinking of all evergreens when wrought into lumber, as pine. Whatever may once have been the case, we very much doubt whether the pine is now the predominant tree of Maine. A lady of some discrimination declared to the writer that she journeyed over two hundred miles in Maine without seeing a pine from her car window. We wonder whether she might not have taken at least a few naps. A surprise, however, awaits the traveler who supposes that he is about to drive through interminable pine forests. The spruce is very much in evidence, fir is common, hackmatack usual, and hemlock more than common.

Perhaps a pine, at its best estate, is the most picturesque of trees, but it is seldom that great pines are symmetrical. The gnarled growth of a pine may be more picturesque, but it is a question whether the pure beauty of a perfect cone is not more attractive. While it is doubtless true that the pine was culled out near the shore, it probably was never as predominant as it was popularly supposed to have been.

The most valuable wood economically in Maine is perhaps the spruce. It is being cut away so rapidly that without careful restrictions the state is likely to be denuded. The spruce is a tree of very great beauty both as to color and form. It is also an ideal wood for ship spars as well as its more common use for paper pulp. In its different varieties it is found almost everywhere in Maine. Evergreens are found more particularly on a light soil. It is, indeed, a very happy provision of nature that pines will grow in almost pure sand. We have seen splendid forests of pine on land worthless for anything else. The fact may serve to bring out what modern science has shown us, that everything can be used. There are no barren soils, especially in eastern America, since we find here no deleterious chemicals in the soils, and every bare tract can be converted into a valuable plantation. The importance of pine is on this account coming much to the fore just now.

A curious condition regarding tree growths is that trees growing in the open, with limbs on all sides, are of small value commercially, while esthetically they are far finer than forest trees. Indeed, a lone tree, left after the forest is cut away from it, is rather unsightly, since it has only a small tuft in the way of foliage. We are indebted to the darkness for the goodness of timber. In the forest the lower limbs cease to develop and leave no trace except small knots. Yet we have an admiration for the beauty of forest trees, since they complement one another, growing in the mass. Their foliage is so far away that we hear only a distant sough. We walk like pigmies among the mighty boles, and lay our hands affectionately upon them. Sometimes, even in the deep forests, the ferns make a fine growth. Near Moosehead Lake we came upon a good half acre of maidenhair ferns, the most extensive tract we have observed. Near the streams, also, either on the trees or on the rocks, within the reach of wind-blown spray, fine mosses thrive, and we have shown a detail of such moss, on the banks of the Penobscot.

The fir tree is not very familiar in the lower temperate zone. Its foliage somewhat resembles the hemlock, except that the short needles grow out in every direction from the stem. The rich color and the exuberance of the foliage has a fine effect. This is the tree which supplies the balsam so highly regarded in the last generation as a pulmonary remedy. The odor of the balsam is still supposed to be healing. Whether, there is a direct benefit, or that better indirect benefit derived from wandering in the forest and living outdoors, we do not know.

The gums of evergreens, especially the spruce, are best collected where, as not seldom occurs, a lightning stroke has left a long seam in the bark

A QUAINT OVERHANG, PORTLAND–STANDISH ROAD

from top to bottom. In this wound the tree exudes its gums to save itself, and affords a fine harvest for the gum hunter. At first the crystal globules are mere pitch, and it requires some years for them to become good gum.

The interest of a forest lies largely in the superimposed growth. The ancient trees that have fallen and gone back into the soil are the source from which the new growth arises. Where this process is often repeated, we obtain the fine depth of wood-mold so stimulative to plant growth. It affords no end of sweet imaginings to see a recently fallen tree lying upon another that is moss and punk, while this tree, in turn, rests upon still another which has wholly disintegrated. It is not often that forest fires have allowed this condition. It is the underlying punk wood which carries the fires, sometimes for a half mile, in a wholly invisible manner. The flame will then break out again at great distance. This is why fire fighting is so difficult, dealing as it does with an elusive element in an ancient wood. The old punk burns like a slow match, with a dull glow. We suppose that the cigarette smoker will continue his vicious habit, until the time comes, as it may in some generation, when men seek higher pleasures than that of nicotine. The campaign against fires is pretty vigor-

[*Text continued on page* 115.]

ON SABBATH DAY LAKE

MEDITATIONS

Written by MILDRED HOBBS for picture on page 110

I

In a singing silence I dream and float,
Riding over tree-tops in a white boat.

The tree things and water things my young brothers are,
All of us made from the same small star.

Far past green shores whose colors overflow,
And out upon the heavens, with soft clouds below!

II

Drifting between two sapphire skies,
My spirit in a trance of wonder lies,
As though already from its star-dust free,
Seeing afar into eternity
And sensing the sublime reality.

I lose the hours until the planets make
Their nightly pilgrimage across the lake.

III

Far, far away among those orbs of light
Live other marveling souls, star-bound as we.
Up-gazing from their wooden boats at night,
Afloat on quiet lakes, perhaps they see
And Venus and a thousand other stars.
The twinkling glow of Earth along with Mars

I wonder if they have one day in seven
For looking into heaven,
And whether in the soul-land we shall meet
Our brothers of the stars, at God's feet.

A SUMMER SHORE—NEAR BATH

AWAY DOWN EAST——DRESDEN

A CRYSTAL LANDING——GRAY

CAMDEN HARBOR

SABBATH DAY LAKE—NEW GLOUCESTER

BIRCHES IN SUNLIGHT—CAMDEN

A SABATTUS SHORE

THE RIPPLES' EDGE

AT LEISURE—CAMDEN

UNDER THE CREST—CAMDEN

THE BOAT UNDER THE BOUGH—WISCASSET

A DIVING POOL, CRYSTAL LAKE—GRAY

FERN, BLOOM AND ELM—DRESDEN

ously waged, by warnings to extinguish all camp fires, but so long as it does not constitute a crime to smoke cigarettes, little headway will be made.

There is something back of forest fires that lies in uneducated natures. There is an abundant number of city people who seem to recognize no property rights in the country. They freely break down lilacs and the blossoming boughs of apple trees, and make use of the land wherever their fine fancy prompts. They could own this earth on which they tread for a very small investment. They prove, however, that their interest is not serious, and their admiration not honest. The love of nature is shown by the respect we show to her. To build a fire against a dwelling is not nearly so dangerous as to build a fire in the forest, unless a site with wide areas of clean earth surrounds the blaze. A forest fire is like a bitter word, left to rankle. When we consider the slowness of the growth of a character or a tree, it is no less than a miracle that we have good men and good trees. The Indians were accused of setting fires for various purposes, in the old days. Sometimes they wished to drive out game; sometimes they wished to encourage the growth of grasses or shrubs for deer and moose to browse upon. But since they used little timber, in their crude civilization, they were not as blameworthy as the present day barbarian who is destroying the ancient forest. Nothing is more unsightly than a burned-over tract. Nothing is more delightful than an undisturbed woodland. We are slowly learning that to call a man civilized does not make him so, and that the savagery of the twentieth century is far more dangerous, and in many instances more complete, than was the case before the days of Columbus. If we can't be lovers of beauty, let us at least try to be decent in ourselves. Fire does not belong to us by any right that we can claim as human beings. Nothing belongs to us. We take everything on sufferance. Even when we buy, we simply enter into an agreement with another man to quit his claim to the thing we purchase. Back of his claim is no indefeasible right. We may get our deeds from the Indians, but judgment on us for our use of the lands is decided by an older and mightier power. Twenty thousand acres have just been burned over in Maine, as we write. The state pays a great sum to its fire fighters, and in addition it suffers the loss of its forests and its reservoir of waters. That a characterless man should handle carelessly the mystery of fire is one of the anomalies of civilization.

The hackmatack, or American larch, is one of the anomalies among trees. Though a conifer, it is not evergreen. The irregularity of its branches gives it an airy grace. We have not seen elsewhere than in Maine rows or clumps of hackmatack planted as windbreaks or decorative trees. Occasionally one sees a whole forest of them, usually on the lowlands.

The hemlock, much despised in the early times, is so common that it is now much used as a cheap lumber, though it affords shaky boards. In its growth, it is often graceful. One of its important values is its bark, used for tanning, though the oak bark is better, and modern chemical methods are likely to supersede both barks, and leather itself, for that matter.

The poplar is another common wood, cut for pulp or for spools. We were accustomed to think of it as a somewhat plebeian tree. Now, however, when we see the hard woods, such as maple and birch, passed over as valueless in the back forests, we must revise our opinions. It is said that a quarter of a million cords of pulp wood will be floated this year, down one branch of the Penobscot river. It is surprising to see how well trained the sticks are, keeping generally in the middle of a strong current, where the stream is of fairly uniform width. In the broads, however, and where the eddies form, it circles about several times before it is willing to proceed. In times of high water, tossed up on the bank, it remains, and in parts of the river shows a definite line of numerous sticks on the sands or the crags. From these positions it is cleared every year or two, in the autumn, by a process called "picking the river." Beginning at the highest and most remote tributary streams, every stick is started on its way by the deft river man, and followed down until millions of feet are gathered at the final point. The life of the river men, while dangerous, is not so much so as it appears, to one who watches them from the bank, leaping from log to log.

PEMAQUID FORT

The workers at this trade acquire a love for it. In fact, it would seem that the more dangerous an occupation out of doors, the more ready are men to go into it. This promises well for a hardy race. So long as men are ready to take up dangerous callings, which nevertheless give health and quick, iron muscles, it indicates that the spirit of manhood is not on the decline. The life of the camp has developed a type. The food is of the best, but woe to him who finds fault! By the discipline of the camp, the critic or the cook must go, and it is not, as a rule, the cook. The quantity of food consumed is enormous, since the activity of the lumberman and the cold weather require great interior fires. We have heard of one foreman who rapidly took on board nine fried eggs, as the introduction to his break-fast. In addition to the meats, of which there are all sorts, and all good, there was at least one instance when rich baked beans were also served for three hundred and sixty consecutive meals. This is the total number of meals during which the cook-house was in operation. Do not imagine there was a change in diet. In putting up dinners for the men who go too far

[*Text continued on page* 123.]

POLAND SHADE

By Mildred Hobbs

All the way is gold and purple
Through the depths of Poland shade,
And the road is streaked and mottled
With a shadow-spun brocade,

While the shifting lights of woodlands
Intermingle, interglide,
Weaving tapestries of splendor
Far along on either side —

Dusky armies standing silent
In a blaze of sunlit fire,
Underneath the gilded outline
Of a forest dome and spire;

Graceful ferns and scarlet lilies
Flaming in a shaft of light,
Butterflies of gorgeous colors
Spreading wings in idle flight;

And a wilderness of thicket,
And a deer's soft, lustrous eyes,
And the brooks of diamond waters,
With their glinting dragon-flies!

O the way of gold and purple
Over rolling hill and glade,
And the spell of whispering woodlands
In the depths of Poland shade!

POLAND SHADE

THE RIPPLES' EDGE—WISCASSET

THE SWIMMERS' DELIGHT—DANVILLE

TOPSHAM BANKS   MEETING THE TIDE—ROCKPORT

INTO THE VALLEY—EDGECOMB

THE ROADSIDE TROUGH

to return for them, there were, in this camp at least, always added a dozen cookies, besides the dessert. A cook informed me that such trifles do not count, and that he never knew a cooky to be returned.

ORNAMENTAL AND FRUIT TREES

THE maple and the birch and the elm are the usual trees along the walls. The elms, though not so old as those of Massachusetts, are scarcely less majestic. In many towns they form a wonderful canopy over the streets. In the smaller places, as Randolph, Dresden, Union, and a hundred others, their great trunks lend dignity and character.

The maple is a favorite, largely, probably, because of its quick growth. It requires but a few years to cast a dense and broad shade. This very early maturity, however, betokens an early decay, as we have elsewhere pointed out. The basswood is in some neighborhoods a favorite. The buttonwood scarcely occurs in Maine.

The birch tree, with its velvety pink bark, of the sort growing in northern latitudes, flourishes in Maine very extensively, though there are regions where we see it seldom. When at its best, it has an individual charm unlike any other species. We have been happy in finding at York and Damariscotta, in New Vineyard and other quarters, a large number of delightful specimens or groups of these trees, which light up the twilight roadsides and form an artistic marker. The great wood piles of white birch are a feature of the farmhouses. At Lincolnville, the children of a family built them a fort in the woodpile, while the buttresses were round sticks with their white rims, and the guns were large and fine salmon-colored logs. The bright eyes of the defenders peeped shyly over their ramparts. We left them as dangerous persons, who would captivate our hearts and keep us in bondage if we remained long.

The beech woods of Maine, always winning us by their fine trunks, supply another source of fire wood. The oak is not so common nor so majestic as we find it in Connecticut. The distinctive and frondlike foliage of the locust appears here and there, and, of course, the horse chestnut is highly honored. The nut trees of Maine are confined mostly to the beech and a few sporadic specimens of other varieties. Beach nutting was the usual excuse in the autumn for a frolic in the woods.

The cherry trees of Hallowell, of the great blackheart variety, were long a well-known product. The wild cherry remains as a pest of the wayside, since it is a dangerous and favorite host for worms. Since the wood is of some value for furniture, a campaign ought to be begun against all wild cherries. This tree is quite distinct from the sour cherry of Pennsylvania, so much cultivated for its fruit.

The choke cherry, so appropriately named, is another product, almost as dangerous as poison to the small boy. It remains for some genius to find a use for its fruit.

The roadsides of Maine are beautiful in the autumn with the elderberry, growing by the stone walls and ancient fences. Wild blackberries grace the spring and enrich the autumn. The upland pastures and roadsides are well spattered with raspberry bushes.

MAINE APPLE BLOSSOMS

THE love for apple blossoms, which has become so evident in the writer's life, seems never satiated. This year has been wonderful for the fullness and general diffusion of these pearl-white, myriad petals that fill the air with fragrance and the eye with delight. To this we must add that by rough computation, carried on throughout the spring, we determine that at least nine out of ten orchards in Maine are neglected, and more than half of them grossly neglected. The apple is alive only through its own persistence. There is no general sorting or rating of the fruit. The Maine apple is equal to any that grows and superior to all that grow south of it, hard and luscious even into the spring, when we so much crave its

deliciousness. It exists on tolerance, without half a chance. Here and there, as in Monmouth, there is serious attention paid to it. We have in mind an orchard that once made its owner rich, but that is dying now that he has died. The juniper and the evergreen, beautiful but fatal, are springing up to choke out the forlorn trees, many of them not past a rich usefulness. If one-half of the skill or enthusiasm that we see in California were devoted to the Maine apple, it would be grown in the greatest profusion and would make its qualities widely known. Emphasis should be placed on the keeping qualities of these apples. It would be easy to prove, by the fruit itself, how superior it is to that brought from the west. We have seen in northern Maine cities, in the fruit shops, great quantities of mealy, tasteless western fruit, that sold purely for its skin-deep beauty, while the unsought, but delectable native fruit could not be had except on insistent demand. The crying need of Maine, at the present time, is first a belief in its own products, and then the fostering and exploitation of them. Great areas in Maine, where the soil is somewhat light or gravelly, are perfectly adapted for successful apple culture. Strangely enough, we note many apple orchards on heavy clay soils. Some farms have no other soil. If apples will flourish under such conditions, how much more might they be a source of delight and profit on those farms which at present yield a meager living. Along the shores of Maine, and all about the lakes, apples thrive. They seem to delight in slopes above water.

We have been traveling in Elysium for months this year. The blossoms have told their silent story most eloquently. They came late, but lasted long, and many a tree seemed bent on outdoing itself. At least, it was bent! Never have we seen so many great branches sweeping the ground. Redolent, multitudinous, aromatic, the delight of the hillside, the fence corner, the gable of the shed, and the roadside, it has filled us with joy. The apple blossom is the most attractive form of prophecy. If asked if we believe in prophecy, we answer, yes. Shall not the intelligent men of Maine protect these blooms from blight, and meet half way this most luxuriant and beautiful overture of God to men?

THE SPARHAWK DOOR, KITTERY

127

Among the hundreds of blossoms, the pictorial record of which we have made, we find ourselves in a delicious uncertainty which to choose. We have therefore laid the abundant feast before the reader. Eat, and be filled! We must, however, say that the view of a gable decorated by blossoms at Edgecomb, where we looked down upon a bay, was among our finest experiences. Again, where we looked up at the old block-house through wild-apple blossoms, we felt that charming combination of youth and age, of which the world never tires. In an orchard in Camden, while we were making adjustments for a picture, we found a wood snake twined about the post of the camera, and within striking distance of our eyes. This is the only instance in our experience of a serpent's interest in art! The poor, harmless creature, he has gone the way of all snakes!

The pyramidal form of the pear tree and its early bloom give variety and a longer term to the white billows of the spring. This year also, for the first time, we have found the wild cherry of use, peeping over its diffused abundance from the shores of Boothbay. We have also made our initial studies of effective horse-chestnut blooms, and have recorded the dogwood in its luxuriant and widespread brilliance.

MAINE IN WINTER

THE steadiness of the Maine winters, in spite of exceptional January thaws, provides good sleighing. The modern method of rolling the roads affords a very much better surface than we used to enjoy. In some parts of the state, as on the fine route from Greenville to Ripogenus Dam, a sprinkler is sent over the road after it is rolled. The result, so far as the ease of gliding is concerned, can hardly be understood by those who have not had a recent sleigh ride. For sleigh riding is the king of winter sports, because it may be so generally enjoyed, and enjoyed for so long a period. We have shown two or three pictures in this work of ski jumping and snowshoeing, furnished us by the courtesy of the Maine Publicity

THE SPARHAWK HOUSE PARLOR, KITTERY

Association. The modern tendency in sports seems to be for a few to enjoy them by actual participation, while the many stand about in the cold. In this respect we think the old way was better. Then everyone participated. It would have been a poor creature, subject to raillery, if not contempt, who would in those days have stood at the side of the road while the coasters went by. Any girl is pretty in the winter, with her pink cheeks. It would have been an exceptional girl for whom no place was made on the double-runner.

While perhaps we strain a point if we reckon gathering maple sap as amongst winter sports, we nevertheless considered it in that light in our childhood. Two pictures, one showing the sap house, and another the gathering of the sap, were also furnished us by the same source.

Undoubtedly it is a good thing to induce city people to go into the country in the winter, though it should require no inducement, other than the splendid tonic of the air, the sparkling snow on the hills, and the winter festoons over the fence rows and the farm buildings. Any measure that tends to call the attention of the public to winter as an asset, rather than a liability, is commendable. Maine offers the only large area in the east open to settlement. Many persons from northern Europe settle in the Dakotas and contiguous states. In Maine they might enjoy the wind-breaks supplied by the fine forests, and the ranges of hills. They would be certain of a crop, and would not require the weather bureau to tell them whether enough rain would fall. Maine has never called on the outside world for food. She has enough and to spare, and in sufficient variety, so that life is still agreeable on many thrifty Maine farms. We have this year visited such farms where optimism was a habit, and where plenty abounded. If those persons who sometimes go under the name of radicals, were to study the methods of the successful farmers in Maine, they would not require to press for laws asking farmers' bonuses. Maine is one of two states in New England where farming is still carried on extensively and seriously, with the idea of obtaining one's whole living from the land. Bangor is no colder than Burlington. Probably the thick blanket of winter snow in Maine is in part accountable for the sweetness of the corn which has given that product supremacy in the markets of the world. Every-where, we think without exception, races who have made good where cold winters occur, were good races, in the sense that they possessed good physique, persistence, thoroughness, stability, and in general, admirable characters.

[*Text continued on page* 136.]

A DRESDEN RETREAT

FROM ANOTHER CENTURY—RICHMOND

OVER THE HILL—DRESDEN

ALL JOY!—DRESDEN

A WILDWOOD DELL—ALNA

POLAND SHADOW PLAY

INLET AND OUTLET—BIDDEFORD POOL

A CAMDEN ARCH

TRIUMPHAL ARCHES

By Mildred Hobbs

Beneath two bending boughs whose blossoms meet
I dream of stately arches far away,
Spanning a river or a city street.
I hear the groan of crushing stone,
The rhythmic peal of steel on steel,
Until a curve of beauty stands between
The blue sky and the earth. And I have seen
Returning armies march
To rolling drum and fife with flying flags
Through a triumphal arch.
Beneath another of majestic span
Sails a departing fleet,
While over its long course unnumbered feet
Pass daily. Strong triumphal arches, these;
Colossal tributes from the hand of man!

Under the apple boughs that proudly bear
Their burden sweet I dream my orchard dreams:
Tiny invisible workmen of the air
Carrying on their shoulders golden beams,
Surrounding crooked skeletons of trees
With every breeze
And climbing up and down their sunbeam ladders.
I hear the throb of little spikes and hammers
Building twigs and fastening on
A bursting cloud of fragrance dipped in dawn.
And then away beneath this glorious arch
I see the little workmen march
With all their tools and floating petal banners!
Which triumph shows the greater artisan,
The work of nature or the work of man?

ATTRACTIVE MAINE VILLAGES

EXCURSIONS ending at the point of departure from many Maine villages and small cities may be made very attractive. From Fryeburg one is under the shadow of the White Mountains. A route north past upper Kezar Lake is altogether beautiful. Roads easterly skirt fine streams, and roads southeasterly pass through evergreen woods. Fryeburg is of the right size, and its people are of the character, to give pleasure in such summer acquaintances as may be formed. The Saco, in its quiet stretches, is nowhere more beautiful than from the bridge nearest the village, though there are two other bridges somewhat farther away which show the stream in much beauty. A great boulder in this town has the reputation of being one of the largest known. At Lovell's Pond, also, is the site of an old Indian battlefield. The pleasantest summer of the author's youth was at Fryeburg, how many years ago we don't care to say. We will say, however, that a week's exploration over the old haunts this summer afforded all the joy of the past.

Bethel is a village quite given up to summer visitors, and abounding in attractions. The Androscoggin shows us here many fine curves. The streams which flow into it are even better. One of these we regard as almost the most beautiful of our Maine discoveries. The location of Bethel, accessible from many other interesting points, must continue to foster its popularity.

Farmington has for many years enjoyed distinction for its quieter surroundings near the upper Kennebec and the Sandy river. Its intervales mark the appropriateness of its name. Its old and notable school supplies an atmosphere agreeably classic.

Guilford is a large village close to some of the most distinguished lake scenery in New England. Its river also is not without many windings, punctuated by the grace of elms.

Foxcroft-Dover is in a region more completely given up to open land farming. It is a good type, if we may use the pronoun " it " of a twin settlement, where a certain amount of manufacturing in a market town diversifies the life of the people.

Newport is a meeting place of roads and the base for visiting the beautiful shores of Sebasticook Lake. It is prepared to entertain visitors who go away with pleasing impressions of an open landscape without great inequalities of elevation. The same may be said of Skowhegan and Phillips. Phillips, however, is not far from distinguished mountain scenery. Saddleback attains the respectable elevation of four thousand feet, and Mt. Abraham is almost as lofty. Wilton, with its pond and its background of hills, is a village which, together with Weld, also supplied with a fine body of water, may attract the guest. Indeed, both these towns have that beauty of which we never tire, the conjunction of mountain and lake. Mt. Blue, near Weld, was for long a favorite resort in blueberry time, so much so that in our childhood we supposed that blueberries were named for the mountain!

Belgrade has become a famous lake center. Its proximity to Augusta and Waterville has been availed of locally, and visitors from afar swarm in the region. The town of Rome, which was once synonymous for rocks, now has a broad highway through it from Augusta and Waterville to Farmington, and its sharp hills have become a joy. The lakes of Belgrade have so many intricate windings and touch one another in such unexpected fashion, that those who sail upon them would require years to feel at home, and even then losing the sense of newness, they acquire the sense of familiarity which is even dearer.

The lakes of Winthrop have long been a favorite resort from the cities of the Kennebec and from Lewiston and Auburn. The road to these lakes in spring or autumn, whether in blossom time or in the time of painted leaves, is equally enjoyable.

Cornish, while mainly perhaps thriving by its industries, and as a local market, is a very pleasing headquarters on the Saco, for excursions, in which may be included Sebago Lake. Everybody knows the water centers of

[*Text continued on page* 147.]

HILL BLOOMS

By Mildred Hobbs

O ragged trees transformed in May
To perfume-laden bowers,
What did you do in a night and a day
To those old crooked boughs, that sway
With the weight of velvet flowers,
Sprinkling showers?

Where did you find this soft, pink cloud
Of tinted beads and spangles,
Wherewith to fashion garments proud
About your gnarled, rough limbs that crowd
Their twisted knots and angles
Into tangles?

O blue-eyed grass, where blossoms lean
To brush your tender faces,
How many fairies have you seen
Cutting gowns of dainty green,
And draping all the spaces
With their laces?

And did you see them crown the bluff
With faërie art and notion,
And sail away upon a puff
Of downy dandelion fluff,
With fitful, dreamy motion
Toward the ocean?

APPLE AND DANDELION FLUFF—NORTH EDGECOMB

A MAINE CORNER—LINCOLNVILLE

LEANING TO THE SHORE—CAMDEN

JEFFERSON BORDERS

FAIR BANKS—LISBON

HIDDEN GABLES

KENNEBEC BLOSSOMS—WHITEFIELD

WHERE THE LAKE SHOALS—WISCASSET

PITCHER POND—NEAR BELFAST

A BURDEN OF BEAUTY—ALNA

THE CAMPUS OF BOWDOIN

A RETIRING COTTAGE

MARANACOOK

CAMDEN MOUNTAINS

NINE SISTERS—TOPSHAM

MAINE IN SPRING—OXFORD COUNTY

Bridgton and Naples, and the features of Poland are too distinctive to require elaboration. We have been happy in finding pictures of fine woodland drives in this vicinity.

We have already mentioned, though our minds constantly revert to, the charms of Wiscasset and Damariscotta. If we were to speak of a red letter day in Maine, perhaps the most enjoyable we have had for years, we should say it was a spring day in and about Wiscasset. There is a little ice pond near the village, whose borders are studded with blossoms, at intervals, producing most artistic effects. Then the drive to Dresden, returning through Alna, supplied us with delightful scenes.

We have discussed already the villages of Camden and Castine, and the attractions of Bar Harbor.

Belfast is a little city whose country roads, though not all very smooth, are dotted by cottages and skirted by farms and decorated with lakes and streams so as to hold our attention.

Eastport and Calais should be sufficient with their waters and their inland drives to the lakes and streams behind them, to hold attention for a long time. Princeton and its lakes, among the largest in Maine, when all attendant smaller lakes are taken together, is the center of a very important and fascinating district.

Aroostook County, in Houlton, Presque Isle, Fort Fairfield, Caribou and Fort Kent, has villages which are headquarters for a study of a fertile and magnificent farming district. Here, in a rich soil and in a strong way, the people of Aroostook carve their fortunes from their broad lands. In Schoodic Lake, and Grand Lake, at the southeast corner of the county, and in the very extensive Eagle Lakes at the northern end of the county, canoeing at its highest estate calls to the water lover. In fact, the Eagle Lakes offer perhaps a longer unbroken water route than any other lake route in the state. All this district is yet capable of very much larger development. It holds virgin forests and farm lands, so extensive, and watered by so many fine streams, that this county alone is worth, and perhaps ought eventually to receive, a special volume. Possibly if we unite

Aroostook with northern Penobscot and the whole of Piscataquis, and the greater part of Somerset counties, we should have a district unrivaled in the world for its lake attractions. The villages from which one could set out are somewhat remote from one's destination. But these villages are largely experienced in supplying the needs of the traveler. They are not yet beautiful in themselves, not having had yet the age and necessary development to secure mellowness. They should be thought of more as points of departure, just as western villages are regarded.

SOME MAINE CITIES

WE shall not enter further into a description of delightful Portland, since what we have said of it is all that our chief aim, rural beauty, will allow.

Augusta, owing to its fine Bulfinch capitol of fair native granite, its age and other attractions, must now have our attention. The capitol is located in a manner to set off advantageously its fine proportions. Happily the additions have been made in the spirit of the original. The edifice is nearly perfect in its way, for the purpose intended and for the state which it embodies.

We show in Fort Western a delightful reminder of the early days, when Augusta was a trading port. Mr. William H. Gannett deserves well of his city and state for the thoughtful, faithful, complete restoration as does also his technical adviser, Mr. George Francis Dow. We have nothing else of this sort restored for us. It may serve to give life to Parkman's histories which should be read here in preference to any other spot. The Plymouth Colony traded up the Kennebec. The Kennebec at Augusta has just the proper width for beauty. Looking up from Hallowell through good clusters of birches, the two towns are seen together.

The dignity of Augusta, viewed from either bank, is striking. Here such brilliant men as Blaine and Bradbury made their homes. But there has been long a line of people of quiet cultivation and delightful home life to give tone to Augusta. Here also is, so some say, the noblest modern private residence in New England. Here a great dam on the river marks the limit of tidal water and provides a basis for that manufacturing which forms some part of the life of all Maine's cities.

As a touring center Augusta has undeniable claims. It is here also that the peculiar contour of the fields formed by the quick dips of clay hills, is seen in perfection. The country is rich in green farms.

Gardiner is a thriving rival of Augusta, to the south, and Waterville to the north, and each is the center of alluring drives on both sides of the Kennebec. Gardiner is the point where ocean-going steamers must end their ascent of the river. It is the site of a home of old world dignity and stability, the noble Gardiner mansion still the center of a charming hospitality. The approaches along the "outlet" to Winthrop pond, as we used in childhood to call the great lake, is to be commended, as well as the drives to Richmond, Randolph and beyond. Indeed the east bank of the river where no cities are, is very pleasing for a long, long way.

Waterville derives éclat from Colby University, and of course the city rejoices in its river power. Winslow with its Fort Fairfax, or the remnant of it, is virtually a part of Waterville, while Oakland is the other suburb.

The Kennebec from Waterville to Richmond is a little empire of fair fields and trim homes of activity and alertness. It is one of the four groups which make the body of Maine's activities of the old sort, the others being Portland, Lewiston-Auburn, and Bangor. Bangor is really a center of all the Penobscot country, with Bucksport, Castine, Oldtown and Orono for its outposts. Thriving, ambitious, rich in resources, open to the sea, the base of the Aroostook and lake district, it may well consider itself the second center in Maine, and the first in natural wealth. The great island above in the river with the contiguous waterways may have stimulated the development of the Oldtown canoe to its present perfection.

Where would one live in Maine, if a choice lay open? A dangerous

[Text continued on page 155.]

BOOTHBAY EVERGREENS

BY MILDRED HOBBS

They stand between daylight and dark on the emerald curve of the shore,
When the heavens are tinged with the sun, and the sea is reflecting the
moon.
They sway against slow-fading skies, while the glow of the cove's tinted
floor
Gleams rose through the dusk of the branches, where winds from a far
ocean croon.

The glistening needles are whispering songs through the rock-clustered firs,
Through the sweet-scented balsams and pines and spruces deep-shaded
with blue,
Whose boughs are the harps of the wind of the sea, when at even it stirs
The murmuring, soft-sighing echoes of songs that the wise men knew.

It must be a carol of yule when the voices of evergreens croon,
While the heavens are filling with stars that are hung on the tips of
the trees,
All festooned with a silvery tinsel and ornaments dropped from the moon,
For the soul of a man they would lift, and the heart of a child they
would please!

BETWEEN PINES—EAST BOOTHBAY

ELM GABLES—WATERBORO

A SPRING WEDDING—ALNA

THE ORCHARD COTTAGE—RICHMOND

A PATH ON THE SACO—FRYEBURG

AN OPEN ROAD

AN OLD SALT POND—EAST BOOTHBAY

question, like choosing a wife. There are many calls and so many tastes that we must leave the matter open in some degree. If one desires the double advantage of salt and fresh waters, without urban conditions, several shore towns call us. We have named them. Portland is the supreme city for all attractions in Maine. The college towns of course appeal to the person who though out of school is always a student. Towns with mountains and lakes near are found satisfactory in every respect to not a few, who enjoy their work within sight of God's work. A river town is as rich as any in the variety of its possible routes, by land or water, in the association with worth-while people, and the opportunity for carrying on an occupation. Which river town? Oh! that would be telling. The one of course that feeds your nature and need and your loves most satisfactorily.

LET US GO DOWN INTO MAINE!

WHERE Mount Agamenticus calls us, and Cape Niddick and Ogunquit, and Webhannet, and Kennebunk. From Bauneg Beg Pond to Mousam river and Alewives pond, let us feel at home at Goose Fair bay, and cross the river where the hen did at Biddeford, to reach Casco Bay. Up Merriconeag Sound we sail. We dodge Overset and Bustling and Stave islands, and make salute at Little Bang. We leave Rogue island behind, and doff our caps at Isaiah cove and Ministerial island. Fearful of Sister island, we run past Flying Point and Wolfe Neck, and up Harraseekit river, or Maquoit bay, to Bunganuc landing. Where Androscoggin bounds Sagadahoc we sail boldly on, leaving the islands, Bold Dick to wrestle with White Bull and Brown Cow, and refresh ourselves at Gooseberry island and Bald Head cove. At Sequin we glimpse Popham and the Kennebec.

Let us fish in the waters of Cobbosseecontee, of Purgatory Pond or Winnegance bay. Let us glide through Fiddler reach, past Doughty point, or Widgeon cove to Hockamock bay or Nequasset brook, coming to rest on

Mt. Ararat in Cumberland county. Let us put in a sentimental day at Loves brook or Knight pond, sailing on Nonesuch river, stopping at Dark harbor, or Half Moon pond, and resting at last on Doddling hill. Why not?

Oh! let us go down into Maine, to Neontaquet river or Watchic pond, to peep through Isinglass hill, at Shy Beaver pond. Setting out from Brave Boat harbor, marking progress at Notched pond, hunting on Panther lake, let us pass the week-end at Sabbath Day lake or Jordan bay on Sebago, but writing home from Inkhorn brook, and renewing our flask at Powderhorn island. Dodging Folly and Rum islands, we shall naturally land at Bumpkin. We have nothing to do with Bareneck, or Spurwink river, as we prefer Oriocoag and Presumpscot rivers, and Knubble bay. Thomas' Great Toe we leave, with Cain pond, to find Pemaquid, oldest of sites, whence away to Souadabascook stream, Alamoosook lake, near the Penobscot, for a real fishing trip, there and on the Kenduskeag, or Sunkhaze stream or Nehumkeag pond.

Let us go down into Maine! At Skowhegan and Norridgewock, in Indian wise we fish, and carry to Messalonskee lake, by Crooked river and Coffee pond, leaping Breakneck brook, we rest at Anonymous pond and wish they all had that name. For why is Papoose pond and Squapan lake, when the Indian lived who named Umbazookus, Chemquassabumtook and Pattagumpus, "wonderful lakes of Maine?" While Pataquongomis and Penneseewasee, Passadumkeak and Sisladobsis remain, the waters of Allaquash, Keoka, Masardis and Saboois seem tame.

Let us go down into Maine! There only on Pocomoonshine and Meddybemps may we fish, there alone break on our ears the euphonious wave sounds of Pamedecook, of Moteseniock, of Parmachene, the beauties of Caucomgomock, of Musquacook and Maranacook, of Mopang and Madawaska and Mattagamonsis! From Rackabema and Wallagrass we pass in a maze to Casabexis, Seboomack, and run the rapids of Ripogenus and Ambajemackomus. We pause at the post office of Ko-dad-jo, and hasten to Macwahoc and Meduxikeag, to Skitiwok, and Nahmakanta lakes, for is not salmon there? Past Nolsemuck and Baskagegan to Pennaquam and Musquash, Madagascal and Gassabias, we paddle enraptured over Migarrawock and Umbajejus and cast anchor in Medunkeunk. At Mooselukmeguntic is hunting. At Annabessacook, Megunticook and Chesuncook all is well done. You know you are in Maine.

A NATIONAL ASSET

MAINE is a present or prospective joy to every intelligent citizen of our country. It is becoming the most attractive recreational district in the United States. We owe it the same attachment that we feel for our home grounds, since most of us, when we do have leisure, go to Maine.

Its extent is ample for all visitors. Its appeals are various enough to attract every taste. For in Maine is lonely shore, lonely mountain and lonely lake and stream. There is also shore, lake, stream and mountain where society congregates. At Poland, Bar Harbor, and Mt. Kineo one may be luxurious. In the camps one may live like an Indian or even like a lazy poor white man. On the farms one may smell the new hay, wander over the berry pasture, enjoy the farm animals and study the economy of present day agriculture. In a village like Winthrop one is in the midst of orchards, convenient to lakes, by roads lined with the elm and maple. At Paris, in Oxford county, one is high above a fair country, and amid conditions much as they used to be in old Maine. At Kingfield by the cascading Carrabasset we may drive many miles, returning filled with the joys of that lovely stream to our headquarters. At Strong, under the mountains, we may revel in their fine outlines or wander over their ruggedness, as the mood suggests.

At the Rangeleys there are all sorts of retreats, all near the bustle of the greater hotels. At Moosehead lake one need not proceed beyond Greenville for a most satisfactory base, with the beauty of Squaw mountain, Wilson pond and the gemmed isles near. Monson, and farther into the hills,

at Onawa, we are in the center of a region altogether good and noble in
its prospects.

In Penobscot and Aroostook counties are camps as well provided as
metropolitan hotels, hard by the freedom of leaping waters and slumberous
mountains.

Who could count the bays in Maine or find an end of those secluded,
artistic, yet accessible water sites waiting for us to develop them, or to enjoy
those already made ready?   Maine holds everything in her great heart
that the weary man or woman could desire — or should desire.

The finest pleasure the writer derives from Maine is not its scenery,
pleasing as that is, or its recreations, however various they may be.   To
talk with a farmer sitting by the open door, in the twilight while the blue
and gold change in the soft sky and the trees whisper their evening good-
night, that is among the best of joys.

A day on a high hill of Manchester, where the great farm house is open
and gentle sounds of content reach us from the barns, this is enrichment,
because it is repeating the experience of a myriad generations.   To talk with
a family who that very day has wrestled successfully with the land, and to
note the sense of quiet mastery, the knowledge of their own pleasure in
their work is as good as any experience can be.   What is the matter with
the farm and the farmer?   Nothing here.   It is a good farm, a good
farmer and a good farmer's wife.   You like it, you cannot help admitting
that here are the victors, here the sane people, who are in themselves the
answers to the hectic unrest of our day.

They read, they think, they talk well.   They have tallied their opinions
by their work, and both are good.   We are tired of theories in this so
speculative world.   These farmers have " all the comforts of home," — a
good home with every modern convenience.   There is electric light and
power in house and barn.   Warmth, cheer, a center for a calm and fair life
is here.   No use to upset the world for these people.   They have acquired
of the world, without cavil, all they need.   Yes, they have good heads, else
they could not have done all this.

THE BRIDGE AT NEW VINEYARD

But does not a successful merchant require a good head? Can a poor head make headway in the professions? Amid all the laments at the failures of farmers why does not some one point out that citizens in every calling fail, and fail so often and so completely that a farmers' failure is success in comparison.

Now the finest asset of a nation is the object lesson of men who succeed on the land. Not merely to keep the land and enrich it but to become broad and intelligent at the same time.

Nations like Rome knew that the farmers of Italy were her hope and shield. Find then a successful Maine farmer and study him. He lives in the northern temperate zone where winters are cold. Neither he nor his are cold. He is able to know human history, to enjoy nature, to mingle in the fellowship, religious or scientific, of the place, and of the larger center. What does he want, at least what does he need, more than he has? His needs indoors are neither more nor different from the city man's needs. And outdoors he of the country enjoys an immense advantage.

So we believe, from experience, that Maine's chief asset is her people who have proved that they can live sanely, comfortably and as good citizens where they are, not somewhere else. There are some longings that prove shallowness, and some that show a vicious desire to collect a living without earning it. While millions complain that society and government is wrong, others, knowing the complaint to be well based, go forward and carve themselves out a life serene and rising. They are then, and all along their road, better able to assist in the evolution of better society.

We are not overlooking the shocking evils, the horrors of modern life. We are recognizing them fully. And we are pointing out that the hope of modern life, and in fact the only hope, is the steady going farmer, such as the one who is making good to-day in Maine.

It is not the nation's wealth in gold or manufactures that constitutes its assets. It is the men that live successfully, and help the rest of us to do the same.

While millions growl and thousands howl the only really successful men are saying little for publication and speak briefly in the town meeting. But when they talk it is out of knowledge. They know what they can do because of what they have done. They are constructive and they hold the world together. Some one has asked whether the delegates to our national nominating conventions consisted of men who had been successful at their work. The question was pertinent. What was their work? "Working" other men? Could any great number of them justify their conscience for the outlay of time and money required by this conventioning? Was their time worth anything? What are they producing? They hired steam noise producers to help their hooting. That was the only production we heard.

The Maine farmer, say a thousand of him in that two weeks, produced on his farm a lot of hay, potatoes, strawberries, pork and — character. We put it last, because *production guided by the producer* makes character. And that poised, strong, kind, faithful character is the greatest production possible and the lasting asset for the nation. It can be drawn on at need. It is stronger than the federal bank, and will outlast Maine beautiful.

A people who can make a state, can tame and comb it, can lift its materials into forms to fit human needs, a people who can make a state we love to live in are the only really rich possession of a nation.

SOMETHING NOT BEAUTIFUL

A RURAL community must work together more closely than a city community. As country communities unite in their granges they may also have religious communion by uniting their churches. One little Maine town has four church edifices but no church organization. Some good man might now perhaps unite these people in righteousness. Either pure paganism — if paganism is ever pure — or union must ensue.

[*Text continued on page* 167.]

LITTLE TWIN CASCADES

By Mildred Hobbs

Little twin cascades—
Dancing maids,
Spreading out your bright
Gowns of white!
Tossing your billowing ruffles about,
Flashing them in sunshine with a merry shout!
Long rainbow ribbons flinging
Into the air!
Knowing no care
But singing, ever singing
To the green glades,
Little dancing maids!

Twin maidens kneeling close beside
The mother stream at eventide,
To her broad bosom clinging
While softly she is singing
Her moonlight lullaby!

Little maids
Of all cascades,
Dance on with a laugh and song!
Sing on and on without a care!
Midsummer comes and it will not be long
Ere you must leave your rocky playground
To go forth and bear
The burden of the stream with other daughters
Of singing waters.
Dance on, dance on, little maids
Of white cascades!

LITTLE TWIN CASCADES—DAMARISCOTTA

A DISAPPEARING CURVE

THE NARROWS—FRYEBURG

A BOOTHBAY BYROAD—EDGECOMB

CLOUD MEETING SEA

The inspiration of some mind, not our own, living and setting forth the higher aspects of human nature, and emphasizing from week to week such mellowness and kindliness of spirit as must obtain if society is to endure, is a crying necessity of country life. There are so many now who almost grow to manhood without one noble appeal made to their better natures that we tremble.

The lifting power of a sane teaching in righteousness is too great to ignore. Country churches in Maine are largely going backward, and many are not going at all. Of course many of the old church edifices are not needed, now that we have better roads. Federated churches seem to answer the need. So few people these days have any denominational convictions that union is happily more possible than it used to be. The person who built himself a church where he maintains worship is happily an anomaly and a horrible example.

In Maine nearly " every prospect pleases." Some Maine farmers have made their farms successful and they themselves are failures. The prevention is some means to carry new visions before the farmers. Moving pictures are new visions. Whether they are stimulants to honor and public spirit and purity we do not know. We strike no balance. But there never was a good people without a good religion. Unless the Maine farmer has an opportunity occasionally to forget himself he will not be worth remembering.

Hitherto denominations have counted for more in the eyes of their exponents, it would almost seem, than character. Those who believe in the beatitudes and ten commandments should get together to keep our rural states from being merely producers of pork, without principles.

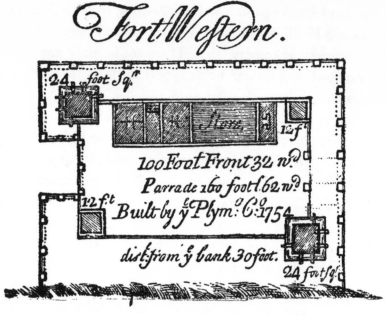

OLD PLAN OF FORT WESTERN

VACATIONING IN MAINE

IF one has only two weeks to rest, how shall he use that time? If one's physical condition is good, he could best see the state as follows:

Coming to the state by water, to Portland, he should give a day to the islands of the bay, and another day to an excursion to York, returning by the same route. A third day could be well spent by taking one of the routes to Fryeburg and returning by another which would bring him to Naples through Bridgton. A day may be spent by visiting Poland by still another route. One may then go on to Brunswick and Augusta and spend the night at Belgrade. The next day he may run to Rangeley Lakes and remain over night. Returning by another route we pass through Stratton to Kingfield and so to North Anson, Madison and Skowhegan and thence to Greenville on Moosehead Lake. Remaining there for the night or going

FORT WESTERN, AUGUSTA

169

on to Kineo we may, the next day, by the way of Guilford, Medford and Mattawamkeag go to Millinocket. From that point a day or two may be put in at the camps by the lakes at Mt. Katahdin. Returning to Millinocket or Mattawamkeag we may give two, or three or four days to a journey, through the length of Aroostook County to Fort Kent and return. By a choice of various routes one goes from Mattawamkeag by Springfield and Topsfield to Princeton, where a day may be given to Grand and Long lakes. Thence to Calais and Eastport, and Machias. If one has a day to spare a northward tour into the lake region where we swing back from Meddybemps to Machias again, will be found attractive. We go then to Ellsworth and Mt. Desert giving perhaps two days. From this point to Bangor by way of Castine and Bucksport. A journey from Bangor down the east bank of the river through Belfast to Camden brings us to an important stopping place. We may have a day or two or more here. Then a day at Damariscotta and Wiscasset and Bath and thence to Portland.

The only necessary variation of this route if one comes in by motor, is that he would approach the state from Portsmouth and have a day along the beautiful coast towns on the way to Portland.

It would not be at all wise to attempt to cover the region we have outlined, in one week. Three weeks or more would enable the tourist to learn more comfortably the pleasures of Maine. A notable addition would be the canoe trip down the Allagash, from the northern end of Moosehead Lake to Fort Kent.

If only one week is available the traveler will do much better not to go north of Belgrade and Bangor.

For a long rest, at points of importance, with every provision for good living, one may suggest York, Portland, Poland, Rangeley, Belgrade, Augusta, Greenville, Kineo, in the western part of the state. In the eastern portion, Rockland, Camden, Bangor, Castine, Mt. Desert, and various camps north of Bangor. We attempt no guide book and make no apology for omitting many delightful and important points because it is given to

UNDER MEGUNTICOOK—CAMDEN

THE LIP OF THE BOWL—FALMOUTH

FROM OCEAN DRIVE—BAR HARBOR

MAY BY THE WAYSIDE—NEAR POLAND

SKIRTING THE ELM ROW—NORTH EDGECOMB

THE HEART OF MAINE—BETHEL

DUCK TRAP BROOK

FROM THE FARMER'S DOOR—DRESDEN

A MAINE PLOUGHING—BERWICK

MAINE SURF

THROUGH THE FIELDS—FRYEBURG

WELCOME HOME!—WASHINGTON

THE RURAL MAIL BOX

COUNTRY DELIGHTS—DRESDEN

but few to see everything. There are at least fifty comfortable lake resorts which we have not mentioned and as many more village resorts.

While there is not so much canoeing following the principal rivers we think that mode of recreation would prove very attractive, especially as it would bring one to many important spots of human interest.

The writer is very fond of small village hotels and they are fairly good.

The flavor of the region is in such places more fully tasted. We have already outlined little journeys from Fryeburg. Similarly from Newport one could take a day for Moosehead Lake, another for Augusta and Belgrade. A third for Bar Harbor, a fourth for Castine, and a fifth for Millinocket. His stay could be extended by visits to Oldtown, to the north Kennebec, and to various local lakes.

Eastport should be kept for a good half dozen boat journeys, including Grand Manan, St. Andrews and the bay to the east of the city. Some such excursion from Calais or Princeton would provide an agreeable week or summer. Kingfield is a center for Rangeley, for Jackman, for Belgrade, and the upper Kennebec.

There are of course those, in great numbers, who dwell, the summer long at Poland, Bridgton or Naples, and others who enjoy an entire season at Boothbay or Rockland. Boothbay especially for water lovers is a very notable center. There are not a few persons, who, weary, of the world's work, remain close to Camden, Castine, or Bluehill the season through. Of course it is well known that dwellers on Bar Harbor never require to leave the island.

Every one has his preferences. The upper and wilder country has a very strong appeal, and there are multitudes of Maine visitors who lose themselves in the deep woods and never ending series of lakes in the northern half of the state, making their own camps and living quietly. It is feasible to occupy some months in canoeing only and never crossing the original track. One may go down the Allagash or the St. John returning by the other route.

A summer is not too long for the circle of the lakes at the extreme north of the state.

When ladies are of the party and there is reason for limiting expense, with a family of children, the thing to do is to seek out some of the good boarding houses. The traditions of Maine people are in favor of good food in plenty. The writer has boarded in many places in Maine with a wide range of charges, but has never yet failed at finding a fairly satisfactory meal awaiting him. Perhaps not as much could always be said for the beds, but brief investigation may satisfy one as to that important matter.

We recognize that not every one tours by the roads. We question in fact whether those who do so derive as much pleasure as is possible by a summer stay in one place. It has appealed to many to have summer homes in Maine. They may there satisfy their craving for the picturesque and they may also enjoy the pure air of the state where malaria never appears. Who would not enjoy getting his mail at Wytopitlock, or who would not rejoice in owning Polywog Pond? The Maine residents are glad to see us all. Partly they enjoy sharpening their wits upon us. The social life of the people of Maine, primarily in the smaller neighborhoods, receives an agreeable fillip from the visit of guests from afar. We find that, about some things, they are so much better informed than we are, the exchange of conversation is profitable. It has been alleged that self conceit is the principal barrier to learning, if we except indolence. There are a large number of Maine people and the people who visit Maine, who are still gifted by that delightful possession, curiosity. Gossip has been very much maligned. Certainly it is one of the most agreeable features of life! If we are neither bitter nor hard, what more delightful occupation is there than to talk about our neighbors? The Maine farmer can tell you just why his neighbor does or does not thrive on the farm. There is a certain terrible justice in the estimate of his neighbors by a frank man.

But if there are those with an unreasoning objection to gossip, though in practice we have never met them, the parties to a conversation may always talk about themselves.

STANDISH DWELLINGS

The man who cannot learn something from a Maine farmer or a Maine farmer's wife must indeed be very dull. Our final suggestion is therefore that the reader journey through Maine for a month or two, seeing leisurely its more important features and then that he settle down on a Maine farm. The chickens that run about are a visible evidence that plenty will appear on the table. A thrifty garden may induce a late stay until the green corn is in its prime. It is a well recognized fact that no nectar of Olympus, no viand lauded by poets, no notable dish prepared by the wiliest chef, is for one moment comparable with an ear of Maine sweet corn. One should shut his eyes and use both hands for this supreme feast. A little butter is all the lubrication needed. The reader is hereby warned however that more than three ears at a single meal are likely to be dangerous especially after the corn is well filled out. We know because we once made a complete meal of this delicacy.

The older we grow the hungrier we get for the diet of our boyhood. What tomatoes grew then, rich, red and juicy, what peas, what delectable wax beans! Is there anything better than a new potato dressed with a touch of milk and salt? But we refrain, for we must immediately go to dinner!

Days in memory that help to make a past sharper with warm lights: A long day sitting on the rocks of Cape Elizabeth while the tide went and came again. Of course we had a book and a friend. This is always safe. The conversation of angels sometimes ceases. Sometimes also we weary even of the wisdom of books. Then there is the language of the sea as a constant resource. The language is not the less delightful, though we understand it only in part.

A day of raspberry picking on Allen's hill. We passed from clump to clump of the well reddened bushes, on the soft turf kept at an agreeable length by the sheep that feed about us. We talked in child fashion of great things, and we ate our lunch beneath a lone elm by a ledge. The white argosies of the sky sailed on through their calm sea. The summer airs caressed us. It was a great day.

A winter day from Farmington to Augusta in the sleigh. The sun shone. There was no wind. A soft snow had touched the fences and the roofs. The evergreens stood out above the glinting surfaces. The tang of the winter air set red blood tingling. The good horse Jane tossed her head and sped on at a steady gait over hill and hollow. Then the joy of arrival. How the jolly eyes of our uncle twinkled, and what a thorough business he made of " filling us up " at the supper table!

Then there was a day among the islands of Casco Bay. There was a day of skirting the entire coast of Maine. There was a day of fishing on China pond. Best of all there was a day of tramping and canoeing to reach the spot where Katahdin is most beautiful. Among all these days it impresses us that none of them included a very long journey. When too much passes before our eyes in a few hours we become like the man who saw the several miles of galleries in the Louvre in an hour and a half.

One may say, these things do not interest me. One who makes such a remark indicates that he is either supremely wise, supremely ignorant, or desperately wicked. While we live let us enjoy learning why, how, and where, concerning everything in the natural world. We cannot learn much now about heaven. True there are those who would try to tell us of it. There is only One who has been interesting on this subject, and His remarks were brief. Shall we not perhaps best indicate our reverence and appreciation by looking more carefully at the world we have?

To our thought the man who, in Maine, dreams of heaven but does not see it has an imagination which far outruns his vision. Has any body half understood the things that lie all about him? It is a grave question whether people who show a contempt for creation or even a carelessness for it are really good people however much they may pray. It was Tennyson's thought that God reveals himself in many ways. Have we very fully and carefully looked for these revelations in Maine? Somebody has photographed the village store and on a postal card has sent its wretched front abroad. As Collier says of these meaningless pictures of meaningless edifices, what of it? How many good pictures can you find of a district ten miles across centering at a Maine village?

To supply this very lack of worth-while pictures we have examined thousands of view-points. Is not our country worth giving our careful attention? The artist in Holland did not have remarkable themes to paint. There is a deal written about the Dutch atmosphere. A similar atmosphere is often found anywhere east of the Missouri River. We have wonderful compositions from the hands of Holland artists because they did their best with the material before them. Similarly, could we have a Corot in Maine he would do much more with its fine trees and hills as backgrounds than he could do with the everlasting sameness of French poplars. A good many apparently valid reasons can be named to explain the production of beautiful art work, and a good many more can be named to prove that such works must be limited in their scope. The plain fact is that the artist will produce results according to his genius and effort, wherever he may be.

Another plain fact is that America is for the most part a virgin field. You many wander in vain in all our art galleries to find a single example of any one of thousands of exquisite American landscapes that are to be seen as one travels. The artist who should have been painting them was in Paris or Rome or in some foreign watering place. He went abroad to study and remained abroad.

The same in great measure may be said of artists here in America. It remains for an American Maecenas to provide typical paintings of the beauty of all our American counties where the material may be found for worthy compositions. In the national capitol we have a few notable western subjects. In some of our other capitols we have other themes representing the development of the states concerned. But where has any state or local art gallery or private individual ever attempted to gather representative scenes of a state's beauties? The omission is a capital error, which may yet be corrected.

The pictorial history of our states has thus far been carried on by the postal-card artist. He has recorded the triple line of poles in the village street, ending his vista with Silas' barn. Within a half mile there was a lovely stream, a nestling cottage, a bank of ferns or daisies. There was "the orchard, the meadow, the deep-tangled wild wood." Did the photographer record these things? Did he try to find them? The owner of the barn would enrich the artist by the purchase of two post-cards, and both parties to the transaction would be highly elated. Yet if this same farmer, so frequently stolid, had been shown a composition which recorded the beauties of his back fields, and had been told that they were better than Holland, and particularly better than New York, he would have believed it.

If now we could inspire a thousand young men of artistic instincts to record the beauties of America there would be a reaction worth while, in the way of sustaining the self-respect of our citizens. Our art schools are doing nothing for us in this respect, or so little that their efforts are not appreciable. They are teaching the pupils to paint some baneful French interior, the abode of luxury and vice. They are not seeking anything national. They may reply to this criticism that art knows no national bounds. Why then do they so persistently scorn America? The man who says that one country is as good as another and then avoids his own country on principle may be a good artist but he is a poor logician and a worse American.

If artists wish to show us the beauties of the world in architecture their field is plainly foreign, because architecture is a matter of the ages. If however an artist is an American as the Frenchman is French he will try to do something in America, and will discount largely the fine gesture of his foreign teacher who, never having seen America, tells him there is nothing in America to paint.

Would not the picture " Looking Seaward " (p. 35) or " Rounding the Cliff " (p. 11), be worth while for a real artist with a brush? To be sure a " Maine Ploughing " (p. 186) may be improved on as a theme, but themes so much worse are common that this might be tried. It would require no stretch of imagination to perceive that " Fryeburg Waters " (p. 43) or " Wild Cherry at Boothbay " (p. 191) are better to paint than a red barn.

We therefore more and more see the unimproved opportunities in America.

THE SETTING OF A COTTAGE

PLANNING the future is a joy which enters too seldom into the American life. The setting of the cottage is a matter of importance. It may be that the next generation of youth, when tempted to leave the home acres will find the beauty of those acres turn the scale toward continuance in the house where they were born. He who plants an oak tree near a homestead provides by that act, which perhaps occupies five minutes, a constant pleasure that may continue for a thousand years. In " Looking Sea-

[*Text continued on page* 195.]

SONG OF THE ROLLING BILLOWS

Written by MILDRED HOBBS for picture on page 192

Song of the sea, buoyant and free,
Sung by the billowing, green-glinting waves of it,
Bursting asunder in thundering caves of it,
Testing the strength of the rocks with their might.
Pounding the shore with a savage delight;
Waving long pennons that glitter and glide,
Riding atop of the onrushing tide;
Tossing their foam and flinging it leeward,
Swirling and curling and beckoning seaward,
Lit by a flash of their own iridescence,
Teasing the ear with their swift evanescence;
Surging, urging the heart to the dance of it
Far and away to the azure expanse of it —
Beautiful, magical song of the sea!

Hiss of the spray seething its way
Back to the sea and the long-hidden drone of it,
Down to the plundering deep and the moan of it,
Dashing the crags with the salt of its tears.
Breathing the pain of the unnumbered years;
Lashing and crashing and rhythmical lull,
Sad as the cry of a storm-stricken gull;
Lone as the tone of a bell that is swinging
Far on the swell of it, mourningly ringing;
Mighty as songs of an army unconquerable;
Hymn of the universe, music incomparable!
Billows that roll with the cadence and throb of it,
Tearing the soul with the murmuring sob of it —
Powerful, masterful song of the sea!

A MAINE SHORE FARM

MOUNT TOM — FRYEBURG

A WINTHROP FENCE ROW

THE LONG LOOK—CAMDEN

A SEBASTICOOK BAY

COTTAGE GABLES—MONMOUTH

BELOW THE HILLS—STOW

HEAVY WITH BLOSSOMS—MONMOUTH

WILD CHERRY AT BOOTHBAY

THE CASCO BAY SHORE

A ROSE GABLE—BELGRADE

THE OVENS—MT. DESERT

THE TOW

MAINE FISHERMEN

ward " (p. 35) we have an instance in which the owner planted or at least permitted to grow, an apple tree at the cottage gable. He already had his view of the bay with winding shore and a never-ending play of clouds. The addition of this apple tree should be enough to influence the growing generations. The picture of it must remain in their minds though they travel far. Maybe it will bring them back to the old home though their feet have wandered into distant states. Beautify, therefore, the cottage surroundings. To do so is to reap dividends in home lovers so numerous that no financial investment is comparable. Have an apple tree at the end of the house and at the back door. Place a couple of oaks at some distance from the other end. Provide a square of elms in the rear. Let the graceful horse-chestnut, the linden or the locust find their places at intervals in front. Preserve an old stone wall with a corner not too far from the dwelling. Along this wall serving as a wind break, coax the hollyhock and the larkspur to grow. Between the back door and the vegetable garden let there be a natural path bordered by low-growing flowers so arranged as to show at least one row of brightness all the summer long. Let there be a seat hewn from an old stump placed at the foot of the apple tree where the garden begins. Then be of good cheer, look pleasant because you feel pleasant, and pray. Perhaps the boy will not leave home. If, however, he goes, will he find anything better? Beside these home charms there will be memories of affection, and the two attractions should prove sufficient to bring him back. We have not over much sympathy with the mothers who are singing " Where is my wandering boy to-night? ", if they have allowed their homes to be ugly. We suggest beauty as a lure to hold wandering feet. It has often proved sufficient in the past. Is its power broken?

" Apple and Dandelion Fluff " (p. 139) is in the rear of a quiet little home. The scene is beautiful in itself and beautiful in its suggestion. There is the harbor, the blossom, with its present beauty and luscious promise, there is the grass and the fairies' seed of the dandelion. Is this not a better place to play than a street full of dashing vehicles? The shade of these trees is even a call to read. The seclusion invites thinking. We ought to set traps like this for our young people. If the home is made too attractive to leave, most of the youth, who are worth holding will be benefitted. Whether they are worth holding will depend very much on the physical surroundings, that is, the setting of the cottage. The daughter would be very dull who could not feel the charm of such environment. It is part of good religion to create a home from which it is difficult to get away. Mill owners used to be contented with barracks for their workers. Unhappily, mill workers have so long lived in barracks that they may not know what they are missing. What a delight it is to find occasionally a village manufactury around which detached cottages with their fruit trees are nestled. For the most part land is very cheap in such locations. It is intolerable that a manufacturer should be so blind to his opportunity as to erect unattractive cottages. Would strikers as soon leave the village with cottages enbowered in blossoms and shade as they would leave a bare barrack? Manufacturers should use the lure of beauty to keep their help with them. We have tried everything else in our civilization except common sense. We have tried all sorts of religion except a simple one.

It was a seven years' wonder that a resident of Fifth Avenue kept a cow tethered on his lawn. Probably that cow cost a ground rent of many thousands a year. There are many things that city people cannot have. They choose their own course. Neither Fifth Avenue nor even Central Park has anything like "Maine in Spring" (p. 99). Behind the fluffy blossoms is a Maine pine, and beyond the pure water of the pool there are maples, oaks and evergreens. The picture is a type of Maine. Its pine, singing its quiet song in winter and summer, and affording its protection on the north, to the bloom and the fruit! Count the petals, note their shading from white to pearl and to rose pink. Lie under the pines on the springy turf. Watch the reflections, broken now and then by the water that wrinkles its face when the wind kisses it. Then if you wish to return to New York, there is no soul left in you.

THE STATE HOUSE, AUGUSTA

THE COUNTRY PARSONAGE

THE good man who lived here (p. 89) has long since gone to care for other sheep. He was mild in his manner and cheerful in his labor. At the country church there was many a one who was called in the language of the town "a hard case." That meant whatever particular sin the person was addicted to, he had not hitherto been weaned from it. It was a matter of dishonest bargaining, or too frequent trips after the "mail." Or perhaps it was too great fondness for hard cider. How difficult it was to hold the people of the countryside to a standard of six days' good work and one day's rest. There was one farmer, who would work seven days. Most of the others could hardly be induced to work six. Sermons on the vineyard and the sower were common. Many a broad hint was dropped by the honest preacher on the matter of stewardship. After such occasions he was thought too personal by certain parishioners, whereas the others were rejoiced that he " hewed to the line." The good man was past middle age, else the parish could not have held him. He sawed his own wood, kept his own garden, and pruned his own trees that we see here. It was the proper thing to have the minister for supper. We do not mean we ate him but ate with him. On the occasion of a clerical visit it was agreed between two neighbors as follows: " You eat him and I'll sleep him." At the ministerial supper the meats were followed by a superabundance of dessert. In addition to a suet or plum pudding there was squash pie, and to crown all, mince pie and strawberry preserves. Any meal at which this honored guest was present would have been thought marked by heresy without the last two named dishes. The farmers were uniformly respectful to the guest, however little they followed his precepts. They knew that he lived the life he professed.

WELCOME HOME

IN our picture with this title (p. 177) stands the old collie, hopeful and faithful. The cottage with its twin trees is a little one, but it is fairly set and has that rare grace in country cottages, a generous distance from the high road, it being approached by its own private way. Such a situation creates a little kingdom for the happy inhabitant. The owner in this case is a blacksmith, who has thriven and maintained his home far from any large market. Washington is a purely rural town. It is just such a town, however, that simple people of moderate property should seek. It gives an opportunity to purchase a country place of ample size. It is so pleasant to have all the components of a small farm, pasture, woodlot, and fields. Only today we read that the population of Holland is very much crowded, but our immigration laws have made it impossible for the Hollander to find an adequate outlet in America for his diligence and skill. We face the question of inducing our own people to use such good lands as are to be found in Washington and other towns of its type, or to allow the European to do it. Perhaps the recent laws to restrict immigration so rigorously are the first instance in human history of this sort. It raises a strong presump-

A DAISY SHORE—MOUNT DESERT

A SERACO CURVE

SEAMED ROCKS—ISLES OF SHOALS

WEST BRANCH, PENOBSCOT

SEBAGO BANKS

TOWARD THE LAKE—NEWPORT

tion against any law that no other nation has ever found use for it. It is popular with some trades to keep immigration down. Is there any trade that would not be benefited by a large influx of farmers into America? It is idle to say that there is already more produce raised than can be marketed. The products of staples for export in America are not increasing in quantity. We shall not be happy until in such states as Maine we see all the good farms supplied with good farmers. Not in recent times has there been such an opening. Land is ready cleared and largely fenced and buildings are provided, and at a cost far less than the edifices themselves would require for present construction. There is something wrong in politics, or some defect in the diffusion of knowledge when a good farm goes untilled. We have already mentioned that the orchards are neglected. Their neglect is more obvious than the neglect to land. There is a broad extent of acres in Maine capable of producing a better living than is available to millions of Europeans, in their own country.

We suggest that a modification of the immigration laws to permit a state to solicit in Europe and receive on its acres approved farmer proprietors would be an advantage to all parties concerned. There are various articles on which there is not an over production on the farm.

The case is not fully met by real-estate agencies that are successful in inducing city people to invest in farms as summer residences. The value to a state of a non-resident owner is open to question. We think that here and now it is better that the farm should be owned by a non-resident who is interested in it than that it should be in the hands of neglectful owners, whether they dwell on it or have removed from it. We could wander for years over starved fields which are neither encouraged to produce wood nor used as pasture or any other purpose. If a new proprietor expends money in an effort to restore such fields, he helps the state directly, and indirectly by employing labor.

Of course the most valuable citizen is a resident owner, such as is common in Pennsylvania, where an intense pride in a farm and a sense of debt to the land is a characteristic feature.

Can the state do anything to induce a love for the land and an interest in keeping up the farm homesteads? We think that a series of pictures of the before and after sort, published in the various local papers would be beneficial. A neglected homestead is first to be shown, then a picture of the same homestead restored to good condition and a certain degree of beauty. Local publications could probably do a good deal by illustrating ideal farm houses. Thus the exotic types not adapted for a Maine climate such for instance as the bungalow, could be shown to be wrong. The simpler earlier homesteads could be taken as types. Farmers could be shown by illustration and by detailed methods how to render brick and stone walls impervious to moisture, and so desirable as residences. This is important because stone is often available where lumber must be drawn.

The use of pictures in newspapers is very much neglected as a feature of interest. The cost of paper suitable to produce half-tones is prohibitory. The only resources is line drawings. If these could be used by syndicates of country papers their cost would be negligible.

The danger to be apprehended in such an attempt is the employment of a theoretical architect. He is sure to attach something to his buildings that adds neither to their use or beauty. The basis of the work should be good old farm houses and barns which have long been in the hands of successful farmers. There are many things attractive to the eye which no farmer can afford to erect, if he must gain the wherewithal from the soil. About the first thing an architect would suggest is a great quantity of stone fence laid in mortar. This is almost always a total waste. The same construction in house walls would be sensible.

A consideration often forgotten is the climate in which the erection is to be made. What is suitable for Pennsylvania would not be wise in Maine.

An important question to ask of any construction is, how long will it last without repairs? The cost of paint is prohibitory. A farmer has an obsession in favor of paint, or at least his wife has. Natural wood seems an abomination in their eyes. Nevertheless, it is beautiful especially as an interior finish, and requires slight attention. Out-of-doors, masonry walls could be encouraged more and more, on the score of durability and availability. Any farmer can do what pointing is necessary on such walls, and can do it in weather when painting would not be possible. Also he can use materials of very small cost.

A definite search for the proper farm buildings would easily result in an abundance of material for illustration. We see, in journeying through the country, repairs or additions being made to very many farm houses. As often as otherwise the additions are made rather to be in fashion than to be useful, and the repairs are of such a character that they will have to be done over in a brief time.

The passion for newness, aside from any merit connected therewith, is the cause of a vast amount of wrongly directed expense. If the money wasted in repairs in Maine were expended in accordance with the wisdom of experience the state could almost be built over in a generation.

It would be easy for a state to provide through its agencies already established, competent advice as to style and fitness of edifices. It would be a far more sensible act than that of giving out seeds gratis. It is true that many trained men are trained in a one-sided manner so that the selection of such men should be based on most practical considerations.

If a sufficient body of material such as we have suggested were published from week to week and year to year, the rural districts of Maine would be educated in the best forms and materials for their use. The present obstacle is the lack of good examples and the abundance of horrible examples. By this we mean that the city house erected in the country is perhaps the last thing that the farmer needs.

If a love for the preservation of the old could be inculcated, the task would be half done. Good houses are continually being abandoned because they are old and new dwellings erected. It is to the interest of the carpenter, or at least so he conceives it, to erect new structures. Carpenters dislike working with old materials. A farmer will sometimes say that it would cost him almost as much to repair as to build new. Even so, if he repairs properly, he may have something of large value to show for his labor. But if he builds it is quite likely that his children will be ashamed of what he has produced, because good taste today in building is not as common as it was a hundred years ago.

Farm buildings should either be well kept up or torn down. Modern costs of foundations are so great that more and more the scale turns in favor of repairs rather than new construction. We would almost hazard the statement that the lines of a substantial farm house built before 1820 can seldom be improved. The addition of a bath-room, by the appropriation of a chamber which the modern small family does not need, and the installation of a central heating system, are needed and are the only features in construction which the nineteenth century has produced of any importance. Of course, modern lighting is taken for granted.

As the pictures of improved dwellings, sedulously published, would be of importance, so also would illustrations of neglected fruit trees compared with carefully tended trees be of use. Perhaps garden pictures would not be sufficiently clear to be worth while. The training of vines and flowers about the dwelling, and the setting of such a dwelling amid shrubs and trees, could be very well illustrated.

OLD DWELLINGS IN MAINE

WE have stated that the proportion of such old dwellings is very much smaller in Maine than in the southern New England states. Maine is a new country except for its shore and lower river districts. The one-story dwelling with one chimney, a square front entry, and a room on each side, is the typical old house of Maine, just as it is of the rest of the New England states. The roof has a good pitch, and the chimney is large unless it is modern. In the course of improvements a one- or even two-story ell has been added. This house may date in the eighteenth or early nineteenth century. It never had any porch, nor was there an overhang roof. The glass in the windows was always small, probably never larger than eight by ten inches, and usually less than that size. The original boards of the floors were of wide pine, sometimes yellow, sometimes white. There was a fire-place in each of the rooms. Sometimes there was a small fire-place in the attic rooms in case the attic was divided. Despite the simplicity of such a dwelling, it has a strong attraction. It is so obviously built to fit a need, and so perfectly represents the early life of the settlers that we find it most satisfactory. Of the earliest period of architecture there are very few examples beyond what we have mentioned. Every one of the ancient houses of Pemaquid has vanished. Even the block-house of stone has been largely reconstructed, and the other block-houses date in the eighteenth rather than in the seventeenth century.

The old house in Maine, as the Maine man thinks of it, is the eight room dwelling with four chimneys, two in each side wall, which came into fashion at the time of the Revolution and continued to about 1820. You will find an example of such a house as we show at Wiscasset. All the coast towns have similar dwellings. They sometimes rise into a third story, although that construction is a little late and is not likely to be so good in style. At the time of the Revolution, the interior of these dwellings was carefully done with a good deal of panel work about fire-places and stairways, and with large and excellent cornices of wood. There was a rapid declension after 1790, and about 1810 we find the rooms very boxy, without cornice, without dado, and with somewhat plainer fire-places. There was also a rapid declension in the style of the iron work. Latches in the later time were made of plates struck out on a die cutter. Wrought work disappeared. Modern butts superseded the large, visible hinges of the doors. Nearly all the ornament on houses after 1800 was on the outside. There the decoration was not seldom ornate. One sees an edifice of this sort and thinks of it as a very fine dwelling. As soon, however, as he steps over the threshold he finds that the interior construction is as bare as a barn. Seekers for old houses should carefully observe these indications of declension in style, and so avoid a rude awakening. There are thousands of people today who are scurrying about trying to buy old paneling to make their old houses older. For the most part their search is vain. Such items as these are now held at fancy prices. The buyer of an old house in Maine is, however, likely to get what he wants, if he knows what that is. The style of house we are now describing is not uncommon. If the edifice had brick sides or ends the chimneys would not require to be built over, but at least that chimney which is to be used for heating should be carefully examined. A feature to be avoided is a roof of low pitch. Constant leaks and constant renewals go with such inadequately pitched roofs. If the searchers can find a dwelling erected before the Revolution, the roof is usually of sufficiently high pitch. We would strongly advise against the improvement of any old house so as to spoil its style. It has a genius of its own, and should be kept to its original scheme or the result is a very unsatisfactory mongrel. The charm is entirely lost by dragging in some feature inconsistent with the original design, and bearing no relation to other parts of the house.

Such houses as we have mentioned may be found along the banks of all the navigable streams and in all the coast towns and on most of the roads that date back to the period concerned.

Dwellings of the sort we are describing are always airy, ample in size, and require no additions. Their four chambers supply as much room as is required because the hall bedroom may be taken for a bath-room. If other bath-rooms are desired, there is often a dressing-room between the two side-rooms which can be utilized. One other improvement may often be added to advantage, and that is a dignified cornice of wood about the rooms. It is probably best to stop with the improvements outlined. The advantage of adding paneling scarcely justifies the pains and the other changes required.

If one contents himself with the dwellings of the revived Gothic period of 1830, it is best to leave them as we find them except for plumbing and heating. These dwellings are not as bad as they are painted. The chief objection to them is the high ceiling, but this is not felt in the summer ex-

VINE CORNICE, NEW VINEYARD

cept as a merit. Of course they are without the touch of good artisanship, but that is to be expected in the nineteenth century. One could hardly commit a more depressing error than to try to change the style of one of these houses to the period of fifty or sixty years before. Should he unfortunately start on this crusade he would find himself spending more than would be required for just such an old house as he is imitating.

One little detail, which nevertheless is very apparent as we approach a dwelling, is the woodshed. The old flat arches ought to be built or restored, and the wood-pile neatly laid up with sawed ends outward. No other expenditure can afford so much pleasure in the quaint and the practical.

It is very common to find the old barn on the side of the road opposite the house and in a direct line with the best view. In that case it is wise to demolish the old structure and to provide such a barn as may be needed a good distance from the dwelling, and in a location that cannot be criticized.

With the fluctuations of human affairs it is hardly likely that the present condition will continue, by which good old places with farms attached may be purchased in Maine for low prices. We have a growing population, and the attractive portions of the country have been covered by their first settlements. It is now time to go over the ground for a second inspection, and to learn what good things have been left behind by the western urge. It is difficult to predict when the resurge of populations will occur. It is perfectly certain, however, that some time, and probably not many years hence, it will be felt that the best opportunities are in the east. We ought to pick the berries that are nearest us. Perhaps those beyond are culled or sour. Probably not in modern times have country opportunities, equal to the present, existed.

A VILLAGE ELM—RUMFORD CENTRE

PATTEN BROOK—SURRY

A MAINE BROOK

A BANK OF MOSS—SOMERSET COUNTY

A WAITING RIVER—WEBB RIVER

UNION RIVER

BY THE RANGELEY ROAD

WELLS AND SPRINGS

IN a country so rich in waters as is Maine, it is difficult to picture the importance attached in arid lands to wells and springs. Perhaps the first human construction of an engineering sort, after the irrigation of the cradles of the race, was the digging of wells. The ownership of a well was better than that of a mine. Battles for possession are among the earliest tales of history. The love-making of Moses and Jacob was centered about wells. The greatest sermon ever delivered had the well by which the preacher stood as a text. In western Europe the stream was too often made to do duty instead of wells. But where a gushing natural spring occurred, the spot was ornamented in all ages by temples or gardens, or at the least by a coping or a receptacle carved with art and adorned by appropriate inscription.

In New England the town pump was first the village center. As settlers became thrifty, enterprising, or opulent, they dug each for himself a well. The ancient wells of Maine are among its most interesting objects. It seems to be the prevailing impression that the well-sweep is the earliest form. We very much doubt the correctness of this impression. Certainly in the old world, hundreds of years before the settlement of America, the windlass well was common. It seems far more probable that a windlass was in use in America for the most part, from the earliest times. We think that the well-sweep was a contrivance quickly adjusted, with the thought, probably, of superseding it by a windlass. In fact, heretical as it may seem, we think a windlass well, at least if it has a fairly good canopy, is more picturesque than a well-sweep. The old windlass often had a balancing stone to counteract the weight of the bucket of water. But the well-sweep, when situated in a picturesque location (p. 80), backed by apple blossoms, has its merits. One still finds it, now and again, in Maine. Sometimes, indeed, the old oaken bucket is replaced by a tin pail. Of course it is well understood that water from a bucket is very much better than from any other receptacle. We are not, however, among those who consider that a well-sweep is the only thing required to give an atmosphere of antiquity to a Maine homestead.

If we were to speak of convenience, and to remain in the realm of the practical, we should find that the watering of the stock, and the various other calls for watering in quantity, make it inevitable, on a Maine farm, that some more convenient source of water supply should be provided. One of the greatest burdens of our grandmothers was the necessity of pumping water. The writer's own grandmother sustained a terrible tragedy by the flying up of a pump handle. The burden of bringing the water, which was often left to the women of the household, was very great. For this reason, the slopes behind the farm houses were investigated for springs, and the enterprising farmer has a supply flowing to his buildings by gravity. More recently the very small charge for electrical power has stimulated the installation of pumps to bring water up from flowing sources below the dwellings. In these particulars the Maine farmers indicate their alertness, and farm life is relieved by this improvement, and finally, by the cream separator, of its last drudgery.

It is curious, in this connection, how we hark back to our childhood, even to those features which emphasize the toil and burden of that day. It is only necessary to think of the things that are done easily today, to perceive in a moment how complete the change has been. All the heavy work on the farm is or may be done in our day by power. It was amazing and in some degree amusing to see, on a recent visit to Maine, the more conservative farmers engaged in the manipulation of the buttons and the valves which let loose the powers of electricity or gasoline to do their work. This is one of the alleviating aspects of the labor question. We are acquainted with one farmer in Maine who has dispensed with the work of two men by employing power which he can pay for, through a week, for the cost of one day's labor.

THE SUPERIORITY OF COUNTRY LIFE

SILENCE in our day is greatly to be desired. It is necessary to the thinker. It can be had only in the country, on a homestead removed far from the highway. We have no sympathy with the city dweller who complained he could not sleep in the country because the nights were so still. The weak point of our physique in the present day, is nerves. We force ourselves to do many things under a handicap of confusion. We pay the penalty. It is an unnecessary penalty.

Pure air is now to be found only in the country. It is a question of a short time before the main arteries of our cities will be absolutely intolerable from the fumes of gas. Formerly, in a city of moderate dimensions, one might have pure air. Now it is impossible. Pure water can be guaranteed only in the country. Some of us have not forgotten the uproar caused a generation since by the discovery of a contaminated water supply in one of our greatest cities. In the country one may absolutely guard for a long distance in every direction the source of his water supply. That is to say, he may have water as pure as he likes. Not only so but, if he chooses to pipe it through an old well, he can have it as cold as he wants it, without ice.

Fresh supplies one may guarantee in the country. No wealth is sufficient to insure them in town. Produce brought in to the kitchen immediately from the garden and the farm has a flavor otherwise impossible to obtain. The milk supply particularly is of supreme importance when there are children. Warm, fresh milk, can never be had except on the farm. It can never afterwards be so manipulated as to bring back what it has lost.

Freedom from fire can absolutely be guaranteed in the country by proper construction. In the town, however fire-proof a dwelling may be, one never can guarantee the character of the dwellings about it. Farm properties are poor risks, since a cheap and an inflammable farm house will bring more at the insurance office than at the real-estate office. But the

[*Text continued on page* 228.]

THE RANGELEY LAKES

Written by MILDRED HOBBS for picture on page 221

Capricious waters smiling in the sun
With the benign composure of a nun!

The birches offer up their calm oblation —
White sisters lost in silent meditation.

A fishing yacht serenely floats upon
The golden surface like a snow-white swan.

But sudden winds, spruce-fragrant from the west —
And the quick waters dance in gay unrest!

They rush past forest cabins in a glee,
Churning the lakes into a mad-cap sea.

Somewhere a loon's weird cry, a heron's scream!
The swan-ship tosses in a restless dream.

   .   .   .   .

The Rangeleys are a sparkling pendant hung
Upon a chain of rivers sapphire-strung,

O what a course to sail!   And what delight
To join the rapid current's foaming flight!

And then over the portage pack our load;
Across the island, on the old tote road!

O life of joy!   To travel light, and sail
The windings of an Indian water trail!

MAINE FARM PRODUCTS—GREENVILLE

MINGO POINT BIRCHES——RANGELEY LAKES

A RANGELEY ROAD

A RANGELEY LANDING

A BANGOR-AROOSTOOK ROAD

A MOUNT DESERT COVE

AN ANDROSCOGGIN ROAD—RUMFORD

ALONG RANGELEY BANKS

ANDROSCOGGIN ELMS—RUMFORD CENTRE

A MAINE LAKE BANK. RANGELEY

AT RANGELEY BRINK

ANDROSCOGGIN ELMS

Written by MILDRED HOBBS for picture on page 225

O stately elms that form a feathery screen
Along the Androscoggin's quiet shore,
Through your magnificence of spreading green
The rounded lines of wooded mountains soar.
Through the cool shadows of your arching boughs
The waters of the river-windings gleam,
Where peacefully and dreamfully they drowse
Down past the village Rumford on the stream.

You are the comforters along the way.
The beauty of your graceful, drooping limbs,
Your rustling leaves, — something they seem to say
Besides the murmuring of river hymns.
Something of heaven's peace you would confide,
O stately bending elms, New England's pride!

householder who really desires to protect his premises, can go as far as he likes in the country.

The country alone is the home of those who would study nature at its source. The great museum at Harvard has a multitude of flowers done in glass. It is a wonderful achievement. A dweller in Maine, with the title deeds to a farm of fair dimensions, has within the scope of his walk almost as many flowers and shrubs and trees as he can ever count and classify. In their soft freshness and in inimitable fragrance they appeal to him. He may toss his babe among the buttercups and put it to sleep on the daisies. Over it may wave the myriad leaves. The sky is the cradle canopy. It is better to live nature than to write about it.

The most important benefit of country life, however, lies deeper than any of those we have mentioned. It is the reaction on our human nature that arises from plenty of room. The most pernicious thing in city life is its crowding on the streets, in the conveyances, in the rooms. The real dignity of human nature is lifted by the mere fact that space about us is unoccupied by a crowd of human beings. It is easier to think on broad lines when we are in the country. We obtain a better perspective. There is greater truth in our vision. We gain poise and the power of estimating values. In this aspect, country life is more important for the thinker than for those who work only with the hands.

WHAT EXPLORERS THOUGHT OF MAINE

ADAM OF BREMEN wrote of the Northmen in New England: "Sueno, King of Denmark, to whom I paid a visit, described to me, in conversation on the northern countries, among many other islands, one which had been called Vineland, because the vine would grow there without any cultivation, and because it produced the best sort of wine. Plenty of fruits grow in this country without planting. This is not mere rumor. I have this news from very authentic and trustworthy relations of the Danes.

A RANDOLPH STREET

Beyond this land, however, no habitable country is found. On the contrary, everything to the north is covered with ice and eternal night."

This was an impression obtained in America about the year 1000. André Thevet, in 1556, wrote thus of the coast of Maine, referring to the Penobscot river: "Here we entered a river which is one of the finest in the whole world. We call it Norumbega. It is marked on some charts as the Grand River. The natives call it Agoncy. Several beautiful rivers flow into it. Upon its banks the French formerly erected a small fort, about ten leagues from its mouth. It was called the Fort of Norumbega, and was surrounded by fresh water.

"Before you enter this river, there appears an island surrounded by eight small islets. These are near the country of the Green Mountains. About three leagues into the river, there is an island four leagues in circumference, which the natives call Aiayascon.* It would be easy to plant on this island, and to build a fortress, which would hold in check the whole surrounding country. Upon landing, we saw a great multitude of people coming down upon us in such numbers that you might have supposed them to be a flight of starlings. The men came first, then the women, then the boys, then the girls. They were all clothed in the skins of wild animals."

Abbott, in his history of Maine, speaking of the voyage of Martin Pring, in 1603, says: "On the 7th of June, Pring entered Penobscot Bay. He gives a glowing account of the almost unrivalled scenery there presented. They found excellent anchorage, and fishing-ground never surpassed. The majestic forests deeply impressed them. Upon one of the islands they saw a number of silver-gray foxes. This led them to give the name of Fox Islands to the group. Sailing along the coast in a south-easterly direction, they passed by the beautiful islands which stud Casco Bay, and entered a river which was probably the Saco. This they ascended about six miles. It seems probable that they also entered the Kennebunk and York Rivers. Finding no natives to trade with, they sailed farther south, where they obtained quite a valuable cargo."

* Islesborough

MOUNT GREEN IN DAISY TIME—MOUNT DESERT

SUNKHAZE STREAM — MILFORD

AN EVERGREEN DRIVE — GREENVILLE

A MAINE PINE FOREST—WINTHROP

AN AROOSTOOK HERD

MEDDYBEMPS—WASHINGTON COUNTY

LAKE SEBASTICOOK—NEWPORT

The frequency of lakes in Maine is thirty times as great as in the central and western part of the United States. These lakes are situated largely in the mountain sections of the state, so that their waters may be used over and over again in the stream by which they reach the sea.

The working energy of the water powers if fully utilized would equal that of thirty-four millions of men.

Europe is indebted to our clover, which was unknown before the discovery, as sowed grass. In the latter part of the nineteenth century it had become the leading grass in France.

Captain George Weymouth in 1605, coasting along Maine, came to what is now believed to be Monhegan. It appeared to him very beautiful. He judged it to be about six miles in circumference. The anchorage was good, and cod and haddock were caught in abundance. Waterfowl in large flocks were hovering over the cliffs. " They obtained an abundance of delicious salmon, and other fishes in great variety. They also feasted upon lobsters and other shell-fish. Wild currants were found, and luxuriant vines which promised an abundance of grapes. They found the soil to be very rich. Digging a garden, they planted pease, barley, and other seeds, which in sixteen days grew up eight inches. This was the first attempt made by Europeans to cultivate the soil of Maine." [It was hot, but — *eight inches!* AUTHOR.]

" The charms of Penobscot Bay and River, as witnessed in the illumination of bright June mornings, seem to have delighted these voyagers as they had others who preceded them. The scenery is described as beautiful in extreme, with luxuriant forests and verdant meadows. The river was wide, deep, and of crystal purity. A great variety of birds of varied plumage flitted through the groves, and their songs filled the air. There were many sheltered coves, with grassy banks, luring the voyagers to the shore. In glowing phrase the journalist of the expedition writes: ' Many who had been travellers in sundry countries, and in most famous rivers, affirmed them not comparable to this. It is the most beautiful, rich, large secure-harboring river that the world affordeth."

" But it was a picturesque scene, as, in the sunlight of that calm June sabbath, the voyagers gazed upon the panorama which encircled them. The ship was at anchor upon the mirrored waters of a solitary cove, far away in the New World. Bays, inlets, and islands were opening in all directions behind them. Birch canoes filled with Indian men, women, and children, driven by the paddle, were gliding from shore to shore. Not far from the ship, on the land, were the few frail wigwams which the Indians had reared. The fire at which the women were cooking, the ascending smoke, the groups gathered around, all combined to present a picture as novel as it was attractive."

In the Gazetteer of Maine by George J. Varney, 1881, it is stated that on the official map may be counted 5151 streams. It is an easy number to remember. If we consider that there are at least twenty beauty spots on every stream, we arrive at pictorial riches unspeakable. Seven of these streams connect interior water-sheds with the sea. Beside that, there are nineteen streams flowing into the sea, but without any connecting streams behind them. What Mr. Varney refers to as an official map is, of course, the state map which was so considered. It must be remembered, however, that this map is largely made up without surveys in detail. There may be, that is to say, on the final maps of the Geodetic Survey, a greater number of streams than Mr. Varney mentions.

The valleys of Maine do not ordinarily reach the dimensions or the steepness of gorges. A very notable exception is the gorge of the western branch of the Penobscot.

In the higher lands of the state a very slight elevation is sufficient to change the destination of the waters. In time of freshet the Penobscot actually mingles its head waters with the Allagash, the Aroostook, and the St. Croix. The Kennebec, with the present system of dams, may be added to this community of waters. The fellers of logs are able to direct the drift of the timber, in many cases, so that it will go down the Kennebec, the St. John, or the Penobscot.

Regarding the elevations in Maine, they may be considered as a con-

A SHEEPSCOT COTTAGE

tinuation of the Appalachian chain, extending from Georgia to Katahdin. The form of the Maine mountains is often conical or otherwise of an interesting shape.

Megunticook in Camden is about 1457 feet in elevation, Green Mountain about 1533 feet, both of these are shown (pp. 145 and 256).

The elevation of Moosehead Lake is about 1100 feet above the sea. It is the highest large body of water in the east.

As to the count of lakes and ponds, that has been confused somewhat with their combined area. It has been stated that their number was 2222, and that their combined area was 2200 square miles. The coincidence will bear examination. Nevertheless, Mr. Varney states that on the maps of Maine there are represented 1568 lakes and ponds. We can testify to having found lakes which are not on those state maps, though we believe everything of the sort is shown on the Survey map. We should count it therefore, an undoubted fact that the reputed number of lakes is not too great.

We are informed that the state laws forbid the entire shutting off of any lake exceeding seven acres in area. That is to say, a right of way must be accorded to the lake if it is more than seven acres in extent. This provision, of course, arises out of the insistence in ancient common law on the rights of the common man. It is thus impossible for any one to secure absolute property control in any extensive body of water, although he may own all the land bordering that body.

Absolute ownership in little lakes has, however, been availed of in many instances by those who have stocked these lakes with fish. In one instance an owner used his rights in a commercial way, making a charge by the hour for fishing. His water was so well-stocked that the fisher was not without value received. Private ponds thus make available to their owner a supply of fish, and the raising of fishes is a minor industry. The hatcheries of the state will supply to a proper person stock for replenishing streams, and this without charge. It appeals to the imagination of many to own a private pond. Such persons may easily gratify their desires in Maine.

THE ROMANCE OF THE KENNEBEC

WHATEVER is the basis of the perpetual allurement connected with "old forgotten far off things," we find it in our nature, sometimes so compelling that the past seems more important than the present. Of course it is easy to overdo our love of the old. Life, however, has a breadth and richness dependent largely on its sense of continuity with the past. He who enjoys only the present cannot find as great pleasure as he who thinks of the present as a part of a great whole.

Whether or not it is rational, it is nevertheless true that the people of Maine derive a certain pleasure from the fact that there were settlements on their coasts before the time of the Pilgrims. The island of Monhegan was long a headquarters for fishing before any permanent settlement was attempted. Residents of Cushnoc, now Augusta, are conscious of a better historic sense since they know that Captain Gilbert reached the site of their city in 1607. The river was long an avenue of communication between the sea and the St. Lawrence. The carries are short.

The Pilgrim Colony, as early as 1625, exchanged corn on the Kennebec for beaver skins. Edward Winslow, a man of education, fine feeling, and pleasing manners, was at the head of this little expedition. The Pilgrims were in debt up to their ears, and, as there was a settlement at Kittery, and as the French claimed the region from the Penobscot eastward, the Kennebec offered the only important water route into the interior. The Pilgrims, therefore, at much trouble and expense, procured a patent for the Kennebec region. Mr. Allerton brought back from England, with the patent, goods for trading. Fort Western, therefore, is not the earliest erection at Augusta. The Pilgrims had a trading-house; and Mr. George Francis Dow points out that in 1692 the remains of the old trading-post were then visible, sixty-four years after it was built.

On the first visit to Cushnoc, Governor Bradford states that the leader, Mr. Winslow, was accompanied by " some of ye old standards," by which phrase he refers to members of the Mayflower Company.

It is a matter of special interest to the writer that Governor Thomas Prince of Plymouth was one of seven men to buy the fishing rights of the colony and assume its onerous debts. Governor Prince was a masterful man who may be counted with his associates the first banker of Maine. The idea was conceived to spread the use of wampum. Prince and his associates secured its manufacture in large quantities and the use of it was very much extended. It became the trading currency through which Prince and his friends were able to pay off their obligations and secure a competency besides. The writer now has the court cupboard which Governor Prince placed in his parlor, the dining-room of that day, at the governor's seat, " Plain Dealing," a mile north of the center of Plymouth. This cupboard the governor willed to his widow in 1673. As it was a Plymouth manufacture it was probably made by John Alden, or at least under his superintendence. It was also undoubtedly paid for by trade with the Kennebec Indians, with wampum. The writer feels, therefore, that he now has a very tangible, in fact almost monumental reminder of old Cushnoc.

The Pilgrims really had a corner in wampum, in their competition with the other fishermen and traders.

A son-in-law of Governor Bradford, Lieutenant Southworth by name, was living at Cushnoc in 1654.

It was from Cushnoc that other trading posts were established which were really more in the nature of outposts. Thus Fort Halifax was built opposite what is now Waterville in 1754. In 1752 Fort Richmond had long existed, and a trading-house was built there.

The presence of the Jesuit missionary, Sebastian Resle, at Norridgewock, of course held the Indians at that point in the French interest, and barred the advance of the English beyond Fort Halifax. Rasle was a gentleman of fine attainments. He was also very faithful to his vows, and was thought of by the French as a saint, of whom the English made a martyr, with his followers, when they raided his village.

There were long periods when the frontier wars drove back the settlers, and the trading was neglected. The old patent was revived in 1749, a new company was organized in Boston, and Fort Shirley was built opposite Fort Richmond. A large house still stands in Dresden dating from 1761. It was erected as a court-house and tavern within the parade ground of the fort.

Fort Western was built on the advice of Governor Shirley of Massachusetts to overawe the French and Indians. Mr. Dow has very fully and with the fascination that marks his style, set these matters forth in a pamphlet on Fort Western. The edifice is of the highest interest, not only because of its historic associations, but also from its construction of hewn logs. It proved an important station for Benedict Arnold and his

SERGEANT LARRABEE'S GARRISON, KENNEBUNK, 1724

expedition in their abortive attempt on Canada. We suggest that this fascinating story be followed up more at length. Aaron Burr, Paul Revere, Captain James Howard, and other notable names are connected with this fort.

Mr. Guy T. Gannett, who was a descendent of the Howard who commanded the fort, has rescued and restored this most important Maine relic, and has presented it to the city of Augusta as a memorial to his mother, Mrs. Sadie Hill Gannett.

As this work is a book of pictures, it cannot enter at length into the romance of the Kennebec, but very early settlements at Popham and other points near the mouth of the river make this stream historically one of the most important regions in Maine. It shares with Pemaquid, Castine, and Kittery the highest antiquity in our national history.

A WONDERFUL OLD EDIFICE

THE old York jail is unique in Maine from the various interests which it stands for. Maine was settled by Church of England people. That is, they sent out the settlers, but the latter were by no means selected for their religious conviction. We find a good deal of complaint regarding the character of the pioneers and fishermen on the Maine coast. No doubt they were the same roving, reckless sort common in a later time on our western frontiers. York was an aristocratic settlement presided over, as was the rest of Maine up to the Penobscot, by the agents of Sir Fernando Gorges. The jail was probably needed. We trust that the Maine people of this day will not think these remarks a reflection upon their ancestors, the solid citizens who came later and settled on the soil. The jail was at once the residence of the jailer and the abode of the evil spirits of that time, or such of them as had been caught. One may still visit the ancient cells and see the slit in the wall through which food was passed. Above, two of the rooms are divided by the swinging panel partition, which indicates that sometimes the rooms were thrown together to provide scope for the dancers. How must the prisoners have felt as they heard light, free feet disporting themselves overhead. The jail has become the nucleus of old curiosities, the outstanding object among them being the wonderful canopied bed, shown in a full page of the author's " Furniture of the Pilgrim Century."

One feels the same sense of antiquity at York as in the oldest Massachusetts communities.

DWELLINGS AT KITTERY

BESIDE the house of Sir William Pepperell, the American general who so distinguished himself, we show the hallway of the Sparhawk house. A carved sparrow hawk, from which the name of the owner was derived, is seen suspended as if in flight.

THE PASSADUMKEAG

A KENNEBEC ROAD

A MANCHESTER WOODLAND

A MOUNT DESERT COVE

AN OXBOW SHORE—SOMESVILLE, MT. DESERT

MOOSEHEAD LAKE——GREENVILLE

A MOUNT DESERT DRIVE

AN ANDROSCOGGIN VILLAGE—RUMFORD CENTRE

There is in the adjoining room a remarkable fire-place, on either side of which, on a bevel, is a shell-top cupboard. The existence of two such cupboards in the same room is the very greatest rarity. At Eliot, which was once a part of Kittery, there remain at least two other seventeenth century houses with very sharp gables. One of them has been ruined in the restoration, but the other is substantially as built, or could be made so. The Sarah Orne Jewett place, in one of the Berwicks, seems to have been done by the same builder who erected the Wentworth Gardner house in Portsmouth. The sign-board at the street corner, the tall slender trees and the sharp roof line together form a very charming effect.

THE EMPIRE OF AROOSTOOK

THE size and situation and resources of Aroostook county are such that our interest in it is very great. It borders the Dominion for more miles than any other county. For a considerable part of that distance the boundary is a river. At the point where the St. John joins the Woolastaquaguam the elevation is about 750 feet. From this point to the state boundary it is 158 miles, and the stream is navigable for its whole length in Maine, of course to vessels of moderate size. To this gradual fall we owe the prominence of canoeing in Maine. This great county is most attractive to hunters and fishermen, because large game is still to be had. The moose, the king of the forest, of course stands in a class by himself. Bear are not very rare. The fishing is still good. Aroostook grain fields are in places extensive, since this is one of the regions in the east where grain can still be raised advantageously. The potato, while a very important crop, is not the only one, as the ordinary newspaper paragraph would lead us to suppose.

The generally moderate changes in elevation have favored the construction of good roads. Ridges of gravel and sand, so called " horsebacks," which mark the glacial drift, furnish an inexhaustible store of road material.

The county benefits from the military road put through by the nation from Bangor to Houlton and completed in 1830. After the boundary disputes which threatened war were settled in 1842, there was a rapid influx of farmers.

The size of this county is impressed upon us when we find it is surveyed into 181 townships. It is, therefore, not without reason that we speak of this region as an empire. Whether this beautiful county will soon be more highly appreciated we do not know. We do feel certain that efforts such as were made by the state many years ago in bringing over Swedes, might be rewarded by a large accession to the amount of population. Meanwhile the beauty of the streams and orchards is ours to enjoy.

The county is one of large farms, and strong, self-reliant men. They are able to develop their empire, but it will be many years before they can utilize all parts of it.

But before the beautiful aspects of the county can be fully recorded it will be necessary to thread its streams and woodland paths for many thousands of miles. The grandeur and desolation of some of the forests is more appealing than any other aspect of Maine. Aroostook is lacking a poet, and the same may be said of many other parts of our country. Had Scott woven the names of Maine streams and mountains into his novels a succession of visitors would have thought the scenery remarkable. Of our scenery, like our other possessions, it is true that we wait for the glamour of a great name before we are awakened to admire.

VIEW POINTS IN MAINE

MANY extensive and entrancing views may be had in Maine. As a rule, they are not suitable for pictures, but it seems important to record some of them.

The view of Moosehead Lake, looking either north or south or west from Mount Kineo, is perhaps superior to any other large lake view to be

OLD YORK JAIL

had anywhere in our country. This is especially true on a day with fine clouds. The islands, some merely rocks and others hundreds of acres in extent; the countless little bays; the wonderful mountain outlines against the sky; the magnificence of clouds reflected on a quiet day in the bay, — make up a total aspect of grandeur which leaves little to be desired.

Views only slightly less attractive are to be had from Squaw Mountain, from the Spencer Mountains, and from other elevated points about the lake.

From the top of Mount Katahdin there is a tumbled mass of hills stretching away into a dim haze. The water prospects nearby, from this elevation, are not so extensive. Chimney Pond, lying almost beneath one, gives its basin the appearance of a crater.

The view from those Maine mountains which are really a part of the White Mountain range is often more attractive than New Hampshire mountain views.

We have mentioned the unrivalled beauty of the scenes both seaward and landward from Mount Megunticook, and the superb view of Kezar Pond and the White Mountains as seen from Lovell.

The outlook from the mountains near Weld is magnificent.

In the south of the state, Agamenticus gives both sea and mountain views, with agricultural valleys in the immediate foreground.

With the completion of the road to the summit of Green Mountain the finest outlook on the coast of Maine will be made convenient.

About most of the larger lakes like those of Rangeley, Sebago, Grand Lake near Princeton and the Belgrade Lakes, there are view-points of great interest. In fact, Rangeley and the Belgrade Lakes, viewed from the west in the afternoon, are among the most satisfactory visions vouchsafed to us mere mortals.

The most attractive river view we have seen in this country, aside from that of the highlands of the Hudson, opens to us as we ascend the Penobscot.

The historically famous view of Casco Bay, already referred to, should not lead us to forget various view-points of the harbor of Boothbay, of Merrymeeting Bay, and Passamaquoddy Bay.

It would be too long a story to enumerate the more intimate views obtained from minor elevations. The hills about the Cobbosseecontee Lake, while not very lofty, afford delightful prospects. A beautiful agricultural region may be seen from Allen's Hill in Manchester.

In the course of this setting forth of pictures there are numerous other prospects which are entitled according to their location.

Among the minor and narrower outlooks we may mention those to be had at the Sheepscot River, of Damariscotta River, and of the Saco, both in its meadow reaches, and in its bolder course through the hills of Hiram.

The Pisquataquis River in the county of that name, the Mattawamkeag in Aroostook county and Washington county, and Machias River in the latter county, all abound in pleasant prospects.

The finest agricultural districts, being in towns with no great contrast in elevation, are of course not notable for picturesqueness.

ELMO'ER CREST—SURRY

PLEASANT RIVER

COBBOSEECONTEE HAZE—WINTHROP

A MANCHESTER WOOD

A BELGRADE STREAM

LAVENDER BIG BONE — BUTTERFIELD

A LITTLE MAINE RIVER

WILSON POND OVER EVERGREENS—GREENVILLE

MOUNT GREEN—MOUNT DESERT

AT MINGO POINT—RANGELEY LAKE

In such districts we must be content with a little turn of the brook shaded by elms or birches. This is the sort of scenery that is found almost everywhere, and is best fitted to soothe the heart of man. It is the near and dear and familiar prospect. It is the view to which children are bred, like the homely scenes of England. We could find Maine people in any one of our states who remember with loyal affection the little brook where they played as children. They sat on the roots of an old maple, and watched the trout, as large as young whales, scooting from hiding-place to hiding-place. The old barway, flanked on the one side by a birch and on the other by a pine, and leading to the pasture lane, that was bordered by wild-apple trees, is a sweet recollection. In Nebraska, in California, they remember those childhood surroundings, beautiful in themselves and more beautiful in the soft haze of forty years ago.

The old apple tree on whose branch they sat to read tales of Indians or knights is a better tree than the most stately monarch of the forest. We come upon an old farm whose owner returns for summers of longer and longer duration. There, with merciful surgery and sustaining braces he tries to preserve the old apple tree, as it is perhaps the only living companion of his boyhood.

TRUTH AND BEAUTY

SAY what we will of the pitilessness of nature, we do not find that the pitiless mood is habitual. Usually she is tender with us, confiding, and affectionate. She humors our whims and allows us to rest or play or think among the charming seats which she affords. Even the ledges in the pastures seem friendly. We hear much of the marble heart. We are not so sure that the sermon in stones is a mere poetic figure. Most of the soil seems to be disintegrated rock, and the spirit of the lily is a daughter of the granite. We insist on our relationship to dear old mother earth. Perhaps she understands us better than we know. Certainly she is honest

with us. There is an unquenchable and eternal effort in nature to beautify
everything. More and more ugly forms are passing out, while the more
graceful shapes establish themselves. Consider the grewsome assemblage
in the animal world during the early geologic period as compared to the
gracefulness of the beasts we have today. The vast, shapeless, slimy
monsters remain only as fossils. Now, if you roam the forests, you see instead the graceful head and limpid eyes of the deer peering at you through
the glades. Instead of the flying reptiles we have the phoebe and the robin.
More and more the coarser forms pass away. Hidden graces take shape
from the rock and from the most unpromising and inert material, life
and beauty spring forth to give us a wonderfully attractive world. In this
sense there is a beauty spot everywhere. Nature is never tame. She never
bores us. Does she ever lay her colors twice alike in the sky? How many
forms of clouds are there? Did anyone ever count them all? Is there
any limit to the possible shapes of orchids or irises? Whether we coax
nature along or leave her in her wild state, she always feeds us with new
suggestions, new form, new colors. Tennyson saw a universe in a single
flower. By rigorous analysis, all poetry aside, we may find the universe in
an atom.

The seeker after truth, when he takes this name, seems to pose as a sort
of twentieth century knight, and to imply that he has before him a heroic
and difficult quest. But is not truth nearer than that? Is not the absolute
integrity of the universe witnessed by the subtle but uniform cohesion of
particles too small for us to see even with a microscope? Moses did not
invent the ten commandments, neither did He who walked Galilean fields
first utter the beatitudes. They spoke in better form what had been uttered
in a fragmentary way before. They crowned the truth and the beauty
which is in the rocks, the soil, the sea, and the sky. They did not recognize
any discord between the lily and the law. Their effort was to arouse us
from dullness and to face the facts. There is nothing new either in the
moral or physical universe. All is mere discovery, emphasis, application,
and illustration. All is a process, conscious or otherwise, of getting into

A LORD MAYOR'S PROCESSION, AGAMENTICUS

harmony with the beauty that is everywhere trying to manifest itself, with the music that has always been in the air in a splendid overtone, never flattened, never harsh. We go about the world holding a mirror up to nature. We discover nothing new, but we are seeing it for the first time and therefore, as far as we are concerned, it is a discovery.

HIDDEN THINGS COMING TO LIGHT

WE may define human progress as a reverential effort to put together the hints of things that we do not see. We are engaged almost altogether in handling forces which, in their ultimate analysis, are subtle and invisible. We have not yet been able to get back to ultimate things. Every generation finds another subdivision in what was before supposed to be the primary form. This is all a most fascinating occupation. Every honest and active man helps. And every living thing helps. The bee does his part. His seed-carrying is more important than his honey-gathering. The bird does its part. The worms are doing their part. They have wrought a chemical change in the soil of the earth. The sunshine creates the green that makes vegetation possible. The wind does its work, and the seeds have their wings arranged to take advantage of it. The freshets carry vegetation across oceans. Salt keeps the world from congealing and keeps it sweet. We talk about the living and the dead; but everything is alive, throbbing and thrilling, even the particles of the rock. Since there is a world of beauty in what we can see, we infer beauty as existent everywhere. We see it under the microscope and with a telescope. We see it forming on the window-pane and in the crystals of the rocks as well as blazing from the stars.

All the ugliness we have so far discovered we have found in the trail of men, who, perhaps, thought they were doing a good thing. Our commonest mistake has been our failure to follow the leading of nature as to what is beautiful. Hence our unsightly constructions, our poles and wires,

THE PET LAMB—PRENTISS   FALLS AT ELLSWORTH

THE BACK FIELD ROAD—ALNA

SALT COVE BIRCHES—DAMARISCOTTA

AN ELM FESTOON—PITTSFIELD

A SALT COVE—HANCOCK

AUTUMN AT BETHEL

THE GRACE OF THE STREAM—BETHEL

and what not. Gradually it is being found that we can do in a beautiful way what we once did in an ugly way.

The theologian has also been afraid of nature. He thought the devil was in it. He has now learned that there is one God in all, and over all, and through all. He knows now that all ground is holy ground. He knows now that the mightiest gift ever contributed to religious truth is the splendid unrolling of evolution. We all know now that the change of a letter in some old manuscript need not upset the serenity of those who seek the beautiful and the good.

The age has done much to lessen the conceit of specialists, each of whom used to suppose that his own line was the life-line of the world. We know now that no one branch of knowledge, and especially no one person, can unveil very much of that eternal truth which is beauty. Thus every great poet now respects the toilers in chemistry, and they in turn respect moral mysteries. Just so that we honestly try to find out about the truth of things, we are all working on the same job. There is nothing little unless we choose to make it so. There is nothing big except as we offer it to be put in its place as an indispensable part of a symmetrical whole.

The only real enemy is ignorance, if we spread that term to mean, as it fairly does, the selfishness born out of ignorance.

SUPERLATIVES

WHATEVER is nearest to us, seeming very important, is therefore important so far as its influence on us is concerned. Moralists and others have objected to the littleness of men who thought their private matters of superlative account. There is, however, a way in which this natural and universal tendency may be counted an advantage. If our eyes were so made as to show near things small and distant things large, it is a question whether we should derive any advantage from obtaining this more correct optical view. Since we have to do most with the things that are near it may be better that they look large to us. If we only select from these near things those which have an absolute importance, our vision will not distort the truth. For instance, an apple blossom hangs over our head. We take it into our hand and look critically at the petals. It is as beautiful as we can conceive anything to be, and, merely because it is near us, we should not, in our broader modern philosophy, think it of small account. The blossom is near us so that we may examine it in detail. It is a flowering of truth, showing in epitome a kind of essence of the universe. A farmer's wife, having this blossom by her window, really dwells with a superlative thing. There are other growths in the little house-garden which, so far as we know, are just as exquisite as anything God has made. We need not go to Burbank, or to those who cunningly produce hybrids, to obtain anything more perfect. We are, as a matter of fact, living in a world where some things have reached perfection. Certain flowers at their best, a human being of the highest type, a summer sky, — all these and many other products may be counted the acme and crown of creative effort. We cannot ask evolution to do anything more. By the examination of various other things that grow, or that men make, it is easy to see that the ideal has not been reached. But we ought not to forget the distinction that has been achieved in the world up to date. Is it not much to say and more to feel that some forms and some colors and some characters are wholly satisfactory? Among so many things that we have yet to do, human nature takes comfort in feeling that some processes of creation are finished. They are exquisite. We cannot ask or imagine anything better. It is by dwelling on these finished things that we gain courage to improve other things. The perfect things are to rest us and lift us and make us capable of going on. What courage it ought to give to an artist or a theologian that he can discover something with which no fault can be found. This perfection of form or function is, of course, seen more generally among elemental things, such as a drop of water or those minuter shapes which must be examined microscopically. Thus the snowflake, the petal, and the crystal have reached their climax. This achievement ought to be regarded as a prophecy. We

FORT HALIFAX—WINSLOW

ought to understand that this process is inherent in the scheme of nature. We ought also to know that there is in man an impulse, call it what you will, that leads toward ideals. There is no more danger of the death of an ideal than there is of the death of a crystal. A crystal may melt and an ideal may disappear from one mind or from many; but the source of the ideal lies in unchanging laws, and it will come into being again. As the clover and the herd's-grass has spread from America over Europe, the forms of flowers are sure to follow. The channels of information increase. The paths through which perfection is nourished and made what it is cannot be permanently clogged. The truly scientific mind is a mind full of confidence in the future. The unveiling of what nature is doing breeds confidence that she has no notion of quitting work. She is going on.

We suppose the atom, in a huge, prehistoric lizard, to have been precisely like what an atom is today. That is, perfection always existed in the primary forms of matter. It is in the combination of these primary forms that improvement is going on and the sense of beauty is being developed. Obviously, the greater number of combinations required in any finished product, the more difficult it is to reach perfection. It is precisely here that evolution is working. Perfection of adaptation is a process, and a process apparently urged by some immortal impetus. There seems to be a Thought behind all. Were it not so, there is no reason why horrific creatures, like magnified beetles, should not have the intelligence of man. In the scheme of things, the finest intelligence occurs with the best forms. The fly is kept down while the eagle becomes large. Even in small things, the process of transformation into beauty is going on. In all large things in the vegetable world, and mostly in the animal world, the shapes that now exist are beautiful.

There are those who fear that perfect forms cannot be permanently kept, since they see how apparently difficult and long is the process by which they have been brought into being. But we should not forget that the impetus which brought forth these forms is in no degree lessened. Every successful combination seems to make more feasible still better combinations. We believe in the Thought and the Power that is bringing this about. The apparent immortality of subtle forces, such as we discover in radium, ought to make it easy for us to understand that this radio-activity is not an exceptional case. Everywhere are agencies of all sorts, immortal in their tendencies. That is to say, matter has a tendency which seems to be a part of itself. You cannot imagine matter without its attractions and

GARRISON-HOUSE AT YORK, BUILT ABOUT 1645

repulsions. If gravity and cohesion and the various chemical affinities are discovered anywhere, it is always in connection with forms of matter, just as character is a part of a man. That is to say, we cannot separate matter from its tendencies or its passions, if you so choose to name them. It is because we can depend upon these steady aims or purposes in atoms and molecules that we see hope for a world of ultimate beauty. Somehow, everybody believes in matter. It is a basis of faith on which all men can get together. But the features of matter which impel it this way and that, that blend two particles or three as one, that make gold and air and diamond, these features may be thought of as the soul of matter. Its affinities cannot be separated from it. This is the most hopeful thing in our day. It means that whatever has produced the highest success, what-ever has made possible a Plato, is an urge that never ceases. It means that if civilization goes down it will go up again. It means that the most beautiful imaginings of a Greek artist will be surpassed. It is idle to pre-sume that since we have waited a long time we must wait always for this thing to happen. If beauty is in the soul of matter, and is struggling to express itself, the result is certain. The common phrase that what goes up must come down, is borne out of pessimism, and is unscientific. The fear of death and disintegration is not borne out by the eternal impulses in matter. Creations continue, and must continue. Beauty rises higher after every destruction.

We have no fears for the ultimate future. If Maine is now a shore fitted to enthrall our imagination and delight our senses, the fact is merely a proof that the yearning, if we may so call it, in matter and man, rests on ultimate things. It is a proof that forms of grandeur of a nobler sort must in every age continue to develop, and the appreciation of man must continue in a similar development.

Wells, in his *Outline*, can see no progress except in a fidelity, growing in man, to the truth. This, at last, is religion. It is also, science. Make the most of it.

THE FUTURE OF MAINE

MAINE, considered as a national asset, is not occupying the position which its scenery, its size, and its resources deserve. Settled first and admired most by the discoverers, it is being developed last. Some Maine people consider the state to be of importance for two things only, in a permanent way. These are its water powers and its tourist attractions. We are far from agreeing with this judgment. We believe that Maine as a source of building material, aside from its forests, must count very heavily in the future. Further, we think that in time its agricultural resources must prove of great value. It will not always be true, as it is now, that farming is the last resort. The extent and variety of Maine's soil will not permit it to be ignored. The lumber resources of this state will of course in time be subordinated to its other features, but by conservation those resources will always be a large asset.

The attractions of Maine as a residence must eventually appeal to many millions of Americans, as well as to persons of other lands. This remark holds true not only of the summer months. In these days almost every one has a vacation. The people of Maine, by taking their vacations in the

HIGH STREET, WISCASSET

winter and going south, will be far better off than those who live most of the year in the south, and can get only a month or two in Maine. The Maine winter is not disagreeable before the month of February, and even then there are many who enjoy it, so much so that more and more Maine is being visited in the winter by guests who want to know what a real winter is. Those who have the leisure and the means to make a southern journey for a month or so in the winter will find Maine a climate more attractive in some particulars than any other that we know. The coast of Maine is the only section of the entire Americas except western Washington that is comfortably cool in the summer. The fog which often visits the coast in this season is a great joy to persons who have escaped the welter of the cities. It always tempers and cools the air, affording the humidity without heat which is a natural craving in the summer. Every foggy day is a joy and most bright days are breezy.

COMMENT ON LINE DRAWINGS

IN order to enrich this volume as much as possible, we have added thirty-two sketches in the text pages.

Sir William Pepperell (house p. 28) commanded Maine troops at the siege and capture of Louisburg from the French in 1745, on June 15, a notable date for Maine since the state — or Dominion of Maine as it was then — was never afterwards seriously hindered in its development eastwards.

It is hard to remember that the English were for one hundred fifty years either actively or dormantly hostile to the French in America, and that it was long doubtful whether the English civilization would prevail. From the Penobscot eastward the country was generally held by the French, and the region from Maine to the Penobscot was debatable land. The Indians of this district suffered so much, whichever side they favored, that between war and pestilence most of them were either destroyed or discouraged, and migrated to the St. Lawrence. There, congenial to the French, they were more at ease though they found a climate still more rigorous than that they had left.

The few remaining Indians of Maine, gathered just above Bangor and on Passamaquoddy Bay, are wards of the state. Their ancestors were outrageously treated. They themselves are with difficulty being brought to understand the independent spirit of America. Visits to their homes are glimpses to a life very interesting to us of the twentieth century.

In the Longfellow house, in the center of Portland, the public possesses a very delightful monument (p. 29), since it was here that from infancy he grew, though born and living for a few months in another Portland house. Between this public memorial in Portland and the Longfellow house in Cambridge, eventually to come into the hands of the public, or trustees for the public, the nation will have very great and rich memorials of the beloved poet. The Portland house being of brick will be easier to

THE BATH OF THE WHITE LADIES—DAMARISCOTTA

ANDROSCOGGIN BIRCHES

BANKS OF THE CARRABASSET—KINGFIELD

A DECORATIVE SHORE

OXFORD COUNTY WATERSIDES

TWIN SENTINELS—GERRISH ISLAND

THE SUGAR CAMP

protect from fire, and with care may become a possession for many generations.

The Campus of Bowdoin College (p. 41) is shown in another of our
pictures (p. 144). Although Maine had no separate early existence, many
of her institutions are very old, and Bowdoin has all the storied flavor of
an ancient seat of learning — the most delightful of human retreats.

The old name for York was Agamenticus, still retained by the lofty hill
behind the town — the landmark of southern Maine, and the stream that
flows hard by. We presume this cut from Drake is taken from a painting.

We are very pleased to examine it, since it faithfully represents the
architecture and customs of that period. York just escaped being much
more important than it is. Only its location prevented the choice of it as
the capital, and for long it was the most important place in the state. The
sort of dwelling shown in the distance on the left is very rare nowadays,
so much so that many traveled Americans have never seen a specimen.
Probably many hundreds of such seventeenth century houses have been
torn down. In a generation those that remain will be very highly cherished.

The York garrison (p. 271), represents the second period of architecture
such as still exists, especially in Connecticut.

The Tristram Perkins house was a Kennebunkport landmark, and is most
pleasing from its fine lean-to. It is dwellings like this that give character
to a town. The fashion is happily revived and could scarcely be bettered.

SOME OF THE PICTURES IN DETAIL

ROUNDING the Cliff " (p. 11) is one of the most charming spots we
have found in Maine. It is admirably adapted in its immediate surroundings and its accessibility for a summer home, and if a residence
here were continued for ten months in a year each of those months would
have its special attraction. The spot is a little removed from the highway,
perhaps forty rods, and it was, we presume, the site of an ancient dam which

has almost entirely disappeared. There is a fine, bold vertical stratum of rock on the left, of warm, rich, brown color. The outlook in three directions is excellent. No lovelier water-view, no better foundation, no region more inviting for wood-paths comes now to our recollection. There are no dwellings near this spot.

A quaint old bridge at New Vineyard, a spreading stream, and a substantial, rambling old dwelling make up a composition very satisfactory to the eye and the heart. We would say that the spot was susceptible of being beautified to a very great degree (p. 159).

In "Danville Banks" (p. 37) we find a surprisingly pretty shore, just out of Lewiston and Auburn and on the Poland road. This region has not been thought of as one of particular attraction. The shore, however, is as good as one could wish.

"A Maine Coast Sky" (p. 47) is a happy combination got by the author many years ago, it being one of the few pictures that are not new. The curdled sky is always wonderful, as it often suggests outspread wings. The attractions of the sky in Maine are often greater than those of the landscapes, in the east. When both are good the heart of man can ask little more.

In "A Woolwich Homestead" (p. 49) is a type of the earliest substantial houses in Maine. A well-sweep still appears. Woolwich was settled almost among the first towns of the state. It was a very extensive town, and counted as a unit with Bath. At the mouth of one of the two principal Maine rivers it was close to the accessible highways of that period. On both banks of the Kennebec from its mouth up for a score or so of miles are found a good number of early dwellings and good farms. The river was the only road at the time. It is highly delightful in these days of flying machines to discover that the Pilgrim Colony arranged for an express shallop, to make the run from Cushnoc, now Augusta, passing all the shore towns, to Falmouth, or what is now practically speaking, Portland, in twenty-four hours. This was fast going at that time. The Pilgrims had good muscle as well as good consciences. They were not anaemic religion-

A READFIELD HOMESTEAD

ists. Like all men who have a living to make they became sturdy, and like all men who establish trade relations intended to continue, they were fair dealers. There is no finer district either for agriculture, climate, a choice of water-routes, and attractive scenery than that at the mouth of the Kennebec. This has been learned by those who have developed Squirrel Island, Popham Beach and the other attractive sea resorts hereabouts.

In the " Old Dennett House " (p. 58) we have a delightful reminder of the seventeenth century. In that time Eliot was a part of Kittery. The entire district around the mouth of the Piscataqua River was settled first after Plymouth in New England. Kittery at that time was called Piscataqua. Almost in the same year Kittery, York, the Berwicks, Portsmouth, and Dover, were taken up by our ancestors. The district of Kittery was most wisely chosen as the site of a navy yard, it being one of the best harbors in existence. Incidentally, the estuary of the Piscataqua is a region of wonderful attractions to the eye. This ancient house has the roof line of that time. It is most happy in a noble tree placed properly as a companion. The drive that we see is the private entrance, so that the old dwelling stands well back from the main street.

We can by no means attempt to describe all the excursions we have enjoyed in Maine. On the shore we think nothing could be finer than the grand cliffs and the salt spume from the breakers. In the back reaches behind the islands we believe ourselves to have found something even better, in the winding shores, the perfect cones of the spruce, and in the miniature harbors beside each one of which we picture a perfect home site. In the interior of the state near a cascade on one of the subordinate streams, rather than by the roar of a great river fall, we then think we have reached an even better location, as a stimulus to the imagination, a constant challenge to activity. When at last we reach the splendid slopes of the loftier elevations in the state, and look out over valleys covered by farms and threaded by silver streams, here and there issuing from mirrored lakes, we exclaim that here is the best in Maine.

Thus it is that what has sometimes been thought a defect of human nature greatly adds to the joy of living. It is a fortunate circumstance that the scene before us seems always to be the best. We can always find something in it of peculiar merit. There is an inexhaustible quality in any landscape. Certain groups of trees, certain curves of the hills and of the shores, certain windings of the road or settings of the cottages, disclose themselves to us from day to day with added charm. It is this capacity for seeing attractions already existing that suggests the capacity for attractions which may be added about the old homestead. The person who loves an old home will often look at it with the view to adding a drive here, a cluster of trees there, a field wall, or some landscape feature that will still further enhance the pleasures of home life. The dwelling itself also may be made more solid or better able to resist the storms. Thus the joy of seeing and

CLOUDS OVER DODGE POND—RANGELEY

A POLAND WOOD

UNDER A BIRCH BOUGH — HALLOWELL

AN INLAND LAKE—MOUNT DESERT

HOSMER LAKE—CAMDEN

CLIFF OVENS—MOUNT DESERT

A LITTLE COVE—MOUNT DESERT

AN OXFORD COUNTY STREAM

A COTTAGE IN RANDOLPH

EAGLE LAKE—LAFAYETTE NATIONAL PARK

A WEDDING VEIL—LINCOLN COUNTY

MOUNT KINEO FROM MOOSEHEAD LAKE

planning must enter into every consideration when one has or seeks a home in the country.

There is probably no pleasure in life, aside from moral aspects, that can equal the pleasure of developing a home in the country. The joy consists not altogether in directing the work of others. The fullness of delight will not come to any man until he takes in his own hand a trowel and lays the foundation stones. Unless we know the feel of a spade and a hammer we shall never fully enjoy handling a pen or a brush. To see one's own thoughts arise in stone or brick, to see the approaches taking form as they did in our dreams, and to observe the increasing grace of the curves of elm and birch and balm of Gilead, as those trees increasingly decorate the home acres, these are joys worth the participation of the greatest minds. To arrange one's own garden and to train the vines against the wall, and to prune the fruit trees at the back door, to follow at least occasionally behind the plow and to see the sod reversed in a long graceful curve, this is a necessity to a man who would really understand his relation to the natural world. By such participation with the materials of the earth he enlarges his range of thought. He mutiplies his points of contact, and becomes a more real human being. If he adds to or crowns these occupations by founding a family to grow up in the country, he has then become a complete man so far as our limitations will permit.

He provides himself with baskets and lunches and takes his family or friends up to the mountain for a day of berry picking. He goes to the river, and with a chosen companion paddles around its curves, or rests in its eddies, or floats on the little lake. Fishing for a while, chatting for a while, watching the clouds and the hill contours for a while, he returns in the quiet of the evening to the old home. Days occupied in the orchard or the woods, where old paths lead, he joys in the fellowship of silence and the forest denizens. It is a good world. Even in the old cemetery, where the shadows play across his ancestors' graves, he is not too sad. He admits the mysteries in life, he meets its pains and sorrows like a man, and all in retrospect blends in one picture. He cannot change it so far as it is drawn. But he is hopeful that what he has done has not too much marred the symmetry of the whole. He is confident that other generations will go forward with a surer brush. Life is good. It may be rich. It cannot be disastrous, if we move along steadily, as we can.

The most beautiful thing on earth is a countryside developed and dwelt in by a kindly, honorable, diligent people. A good neighbor means more in the country than elsewhere. Character shines with a more pleasing luster in the country. There, four or five roads leading here and there in a neighborhood and occupied by dwellings each with its own bass-wood or pine or pear trees, furnish forth a neighborhood adequate for all human events. It is a sufficient scene for Mrs. Wilkins. A well developed neighborhood of this sort supplies the reaction of man to nature so that each appears to the best advantage. We find it difficult to separate Washington from Mt. Vernon. Because the English could not separate him from his home acres they said he was only a country squire. That country squire foundation enabled him to be Washington. The same foundation gave us a Hampden. Putman came up from such a neighborhood, and Cooper, and how many more! But it is not necessary that one's name should appear in any history to establish proof of a successful life. Much that is bitter has been written regarding the inscriptions on grave-stones. No doubt those who carve the stones desire to say something kind. Why should it be otherwise? Are we heartless enough to look for a critical comment on a grave-stone? Why has not some one complained that the patience and the toil and the hopefulness of those who rest in the country churchyard are not more fully recorded above them? Count the stones which they picked, if you can, and the wall which they builded. See their monuments in the solid dams and the barn foundations. See them in the rows of maples and elms and in the old orchards. See them in the eyes of their children of the fourth and fifth generation, those children who have become the leaders in the mighty work of modern America. We reverence any man who has worked long and faithfully, who has believed in his home acres, who has lived with his wife and loved her always, who has brought up children to believe in

THE TRISTRAM PERKINS HOUSE

A STREET IN UNION

honor and diligence. He who has done this is better than a genius because he has been the strength of human society. However America may be living today, it rests on a foundation of men who told the truth and ploughed the soil and fought the storms and fell fighting in their tracks. We would trust a calloused hand, with somewhat gnarled fingers, much more readily than the man's hand that has just come from a manicure. The state is built on truth and muscle and hope, not on compliments and cosmetics.

At last only that natural beauty is attractive which can be enjoyed by decent people. Those who are not building up the country can neither fully enjoy its scenery, nor have they a right to do so. There cannot possibly be a full response in their natures to the finer and stronger elements of a landscape. Something of the rock, something of the mountain, something of the fullness of the lake waters, must enter into the nature of the man or he cannot see and feel these things properly. He therefore finds when he goes away for the summer his chief enjoyment in the skulking rooms of hotels, in the underworld which supplies his appetites by scoffing the law. No country place is good to him that is without a green table or a red liquid or purple morals. We have heard and seen so much of "going into the country" from those whose only purpose is to make a slimy trail that we turn with joy to the finer and more real things. Life in its larger riches is found under the oak and by the fireside, in the sweet intercourse with sane persons who know how to rest because they know how to work.

ACKNOWLEDGMENTS

WE are indebted to the Maine Publicity Association for the surf scene with the four-masted schooner and the lighthouse (p. 14).

The anemone cave on Ocean Drive, Bar Harbor (p. 193) is supplied by the Maine Publicity Association. A picture of seagulls (p. 14) from the same source was from McDougall & Keefe, Boothbay Harbor.

The ski jumper shows Victor Mortenson of the Nansen Ski Club making a leap of seventy-six feet, (p. 36).

The attractive picture of a lonely sail (p. 70) is in Casco Bay. It is supplied by the Publicity Association.

A harbor view of Eastport, called "The Tow" (p. 194), shows the lines of smacks being taken out to sea.

Eagle Lake, at Lafayette National Park, supplied like the above by the Maine Publicity Association, shows the source of the water supply of Bar Harbor, and the mountains are Pemetic, the Bubbles and Sargent (p. 288). The gentlemen fishing are on Stony Creek, near South Paris, Maine, (p. 194). Gathering Sap (p. 18), the little wood hut where sap is boiled (p. 278), and Going with Daddy (p. 36), are supplied from the same source.

We presume that Winter Sports (p. 68) is at Damariscotta. A similar picture was made there by Lindsay, of Newcastle.

"For the Open Sea" (p. 24) is also a gift from McDougall & Keefe, Boothbay Harbor.

Labbie's Studio, of Wiscasset and Bar Harbor, has also supplied two marines, (pp. 165 and 172).

Of the line drawings, The Pemaquid Block House is by Lindsay, of Newcastle. The Fort Western Plan and sketch are supplied by Wm. H. Gannett, a descendent of Capt. Winslow, the commander of the old fort. The Capitol is supplied by the Maine Publicity Association; Larrabee's Garrison and the York Garrison House are from Abbott's "History of Maine," the York Jail sketch was supplied by that museum, and the Lord Mayor's Procession and the Tristam Perkins House are from the volume by Drake, the "Pine Tree Coast." The sketches of Drake Island at Great Chebeague are by Mr. C. N. Sladen, of Newtonville. The other nineteen are from photographs by the author.

In general, the pictures are by the author, and most of them have been made in this very year of grace, so that they now appear for the first time.

MAINE

By Mildred Hobbs

Bloom-arbored, hundred-harbored,
Glorious state of Maine,
All the joys of nature lie
In your domain.

Pine-sheltered, ocean-weltered,
Rocky, rugged coast,
Calling all with out-flung arms —
An eager host!

Lake-dreaming, river-streaming
Land of rod and reel!
Bass and trout and salmon pools
Your depths conceal!

Shooting rapids in a bark
Which nothing daunts,
To deer-leaping, cat-creeping,
Shadowed forest haunts!

Star-brushing, spirit-hushing,
Lichen-covered peaks,
From your soverign heights a voice
Eternal speaks.

Vagrant longings call us back
To you again,
O bloom-arbored, hundred-harbored,
Dear old state of Maine!

INDEX